CW00499803

TINPLATE IN WALES

To my good friend
David & Joan.

Alan John.
December 2010.

TINPLATE IN WALES

by

Alun John Richards

First published in 2008

ISBN: 978-1-84524-125-4

Cover design: Sian Parri

Published by
Llygad Gwalch, Ysgubor Plas, Llwyndyrys,
Pwllheli, Gwynedd LL53 6NG
01758 750432 01758 750438
llyfrau@carreg-gwalch.com
Web site: www.carreg-gwalch.com

Contents

Introduction

Tin or more properly tinplate, or even more properly, 'Tinned Plate' has had a bad press. 'Tinny,' Tin pot', 'Tin can' and even the word tin itself has connotations of inferiority. Tone-deaf persons are described as having a 'Tin ear' and prosthetic limbs have been called 'Tin legs'. The most scornful epithet for Henry Ford's Model T was 'Tin Lizzie' and today protagonists of open-topped motoring refer to saloons scornfully as 'Tin tops'. One must admit that to describe a curtain, lady or Duke not as iron but as tin would lack redolence, although the Iron Duke was in fact addicted to tinned beef. (Beef Wellington, you might say?).

Tinplate was a victim of its own success, becoming such a universal material, and eventually so efficiently produced that its perceived value became debased.

Its use was not of course confined to disposable cans. Picture the Waltzing Matilda 'Jolly Swagman' eating by a 'Billabong', or Stanley and Livingstone enjoying a meal together after the famous handshake. Or the womenfolk preparing food within the wagon circle, the sun sinking into the blue shimmer of the distant Rockies while the men stand lookout for marauding Indians. Or the cowhand, or maybe gaucho, or perhaps the ever-optimistic gold prospector, heating and eating (canned) pork and beans. All with vessels and platters made from tinplate.

Or the missionary, his cassock and comestibles, protected from the marauding termites in tinplate-lined boxes. Nearer home, in some great mansion, the under-parlour maid in her frigid attic, clasping to her bosom a Tintype likeness of a swain, her worldly goods under the bed in the proverbial 'Tin Trunk'.

Or again, Imagine the memsahibs summering in Simla under the swish of the punka, handing round the Huntley and Palmers, (in 1830 one of the first products to be retailed in tinplate) or the Resident in the Straits Settlements dining with just his dinner jacket for company trying to make aged bovine flesh half-palatable with Coleman's Mustard, or the sailor on Burma Station, taking a drag at his Woodbine as 'The dawn comes up like thunder outer China crost the Bay'. All these goods arriving as fresh as they day they were packed at Reading, Norwich or Bristol, thanks to tinplate.

Just as Beanz meanz Heinz, the food-can means tinplate and for two centuries and more tinplate meant Welsh Tinplate. And every variety of food has been canned in peace and in war. It was said in two world wars that Messrs Maconochie and Crosse & Blackwell made victory inevitable. Drink also; the beer can (invented in Llanelli) has become the football hooligans' missile of choice and the Tinnie has almost displaced the kangaroo as an Australian emblem. And nowadays canned pet food is as big a business as its human counterpart.

The British Empire was won by soldiery sustained by *Boeuf Bouilli* [Bully Beef], smartened by Cherry Blossom and Brasso, all contained in tinplate, as indeed were sometimes their munitions. That same material held and still holds every kind of oil and unction connected with engineering and transport. Mansion polish and Zebo may no longer be found in kitchen cabinets, but their aerosol equivalents, equally tinplate encased, certainly are. Cosmetics and their sometimes consequent requirement contraceptives, have been sold in tinplate containers and until the advent of the plastic bottle, tinplate carried fresh water to remote and road-less places.

Tinplate has been a substitute for slates or tiles, its lightness and hence the lightness of the rafters and battens, making it an ideal roofing material in remote locations. Also in not so remote locations when cladding complex shapes; the bulbous spires of the Haute-Savoie churches of Combloux and Hauteluce being examples of this. Tinplate was also used in parts of Wales to clad worn out thatch. This use of primary plate, is outdone in primitive, and not so primitive places by cladding with discarded tin cans. Tinplate and terne plate [lead or lead/tin coated iron or steel] were also used to protect tinplate itself, lining the elm tinplate boxes for the long voyages, particularly by sailing ship, to Antipodean and Pacific destinations. Some uses border on the bizarre – expats can on their birthdays, savour a whiff of canned air from their homeland. Even ladies' intimate apparel has been marketed in tinplate canisters.

Tinplate often figures as a substrate for vernacular art in the tinning districts, but eminent artists have used this flat, permanent and cheap material. Goya certainly used it and his 1790s works on tinplate are rated as some of his best small work. It has been asserted that he used Welsh material, although by that time there was export to Spain, it is impossible to identify Goya's source, although any Welsh tinplate man would assert that tinplate from any other source but his own native works, would not have been good enough!

Tinplate developed in Welsh valleys due to the presence of water for power and for process, of timber for fuel and forges to produce substrate, equidistant between the industrial Midlands and Bristol.

The early 20th century saw Wales' primacy eroded as more and more countries commenced indigenous manufacture. The mid 20th century saw tinplate challenged by plastics, aluminium and die casting, and even that most paradoxical of materials – tin-free tinplate and indeed by deep freezing and freeze drying replacing the vacuum in food preservation, besides which the global availability of fresh produce has reduced the need to preserve food in the first place.

Whilst this book is primarily interested in tinplate manufacture, it is impossible not to mention the technically similar, or even the same works producing terne plate, black plate [uncoated iron or steel sheet] and galvanised sheet [zinc (spelter) coated]. Nor can one entirely ignore the ironworks, forges and steelworks that produced the substrate material. Plus one must refer to some of the canister, hollowware and other manufactures that utilised these work's products locally.

Spelling.

- Where a place is referred to, the correct phonetical spelling is used, e.g. Llanelli. Where a works is cited the original (possibly anglicised) spelling is used.

Thanks to
John Edwards
Twm Elias
Robert Prothereo Jones
Sir David Miers
Charles Miers
Keith Morgan
Llantrisant and District Local History Society.
Various Public Sources but especially the staffs of -
Carmarthen Record Office
Llanelli Reference Library.
Royal Institution of South Wales
South Wales Miners' Library.
West Glamorgan Archive Services

Alun John Richards

A native of Swansea and a sheet metal engineer by profession, Alun John was as technical director of Kerswell (Metals) Ltd responsible for several developments in food can manufacture, tinplate manipulation and roll reconditioning. He was a director of E. H. Brooke Ltd, tin brokers and was also associated with W. G. Trench Ltd, suppliers of chemicals to the tinplate industry.

Abridged Bibliography

A History of the Trade in Tin, Flower, P.W. 1880
The Origin & Progress of the Manufacture of Tinplates, Flower, P.W. 1885
Tinplate, its Rise, Progress and Future, Bowen, J.L. 1894
Monograph on the Tinplate Works in Great Britain, Brooke, E.H. 1932
Tinplate, Brown, W.R. 1936
Chronology of the Tinplate Works of Great Britain, Brooke, E.H. 1944
Tinplate, Hoare & Hedges 1945
Appendix to Chronology 1665-1949, Brooke, E.H. 1949
Industrial South Wales 1750-1919, (Ed) Minchinton, W.E. 1969
The Tin Workers, Evans, T. 1974
Kidwelly Tinplate Works: a History, Morris, W.H. 1987
The Book of Thomas Job, Brimley, Bliss 1988
Chronicle of Cadoxton, Tucker, K. 1991
Tinopolis, (Ed) Edwards, John 1995
Twenty by Fourteen, Jenkins, Paul 1995
Llanelli, Story of a Town, Edwards, John 2001
The Industrial and Maritime History of Llanelli and Burry Port, Craig, R.S. Protheroe Jones, R, Symons, M.V. 2002
Old Llanelly, Innes, John 2005

1

In the Beginning

Although it became very much a Welsh industry, with almost all the British production and a goodly share of world production, being in Wales, (overwhelmingly in south Wales); the coating of base metals with tin is an imported technique.

Protecting small ferrous, copper and bronze items from oxidation by dipping them in molten tin has been a common practice down the centuries from possibly 1000 BC.

In modern times electro-deposited nickel, cadmium or chromium has served the same purpose, but in Victorian times, hearth ornaments were sometimes made of iron, tin-dipped as a cheap alternative to brass.

Cornwall seems to have come into the picture in the 5th century BC when Herotodus refers to the Casserties – isles to the far west, clearly referring to the British Isles as source of Casserite (Tin oxide).

The technique of producing thin sheets and coating them with tin as a semi-finished product capable of being fashioned into consumer goods was probably developed in mediaeval times. Certainly by the 15th century, household articles such as plates, bowls and so on were being fabricated from tinplate in and around Crooked Lane in London using material imported from Bohemia, where from at least the 14th century its manufacture had been an established industry. It is said that the process had been developed there by a Cornish tin miner fleeing retribution for some serious offence, thus creating a market for Cornish tin, whose uses had hitherto been largely confined to alloying it with copper to make bronze. Some tinplate was made in Sweden and possibly elsewhere but production remained firmly concentrated in what is now south and eastern Germany.

The makers of 'Crooked Lane Ware' received an unexpected fillip in the late 16th century when it was ordained that as an anti-footpad measure, householders were to hang a 'lanthorn' outside their doors. A large market thus developed for tinplate lanterns.

The outbreak of the Thirty-years War in 1618 caused interruptions in the Saxon and Bavarian supply of tinplate, so attempts were made in France and indeed in Britain to fill the gap, but the German tinners maintained their grip on the trade partly by devising uses for tinplate, later becoming supreme in the making of for instance tinplate toys, a market in which they dominated into the 20th century. Despite the difficulties, tinplate made inroads in Britain into the tankard and platter market, undercutting pewter that traditionally held sway between aristocratic silver and peasant wood, causing the pewterers great dismay.

The Civil War and the Commonwealth were not conducive to enterprise but immediately following the restoration of Charles II in 1660 the development of British tinplate manufacture was seriously addressed. A patent was granted in 1661 to Dud Dudley (Said to be the first man to successfully smelt iron with coke) and William Chamberlayne, who may have had the idea some years before but due to Dudley's imprisonment (and near execution) as a Royalist officer and Chamberlayne's association with Charles I; filing was presumably delayed until the throne was again regally occupied. Although this patent (which cited steel, copper and brass, in addition to iron, as substrates), was renewed in 1673, it does not seem to have been exploited.

The first British commercial tinning is attributed to Andrew Yarranton who made two visits to Dresden in the 1660s to learn the secrets of tinning, apparently sponsored by a group of Midlands industrialists, who significantly included Sir Samuel and Sir Timothy Baldwin, a name that would later loom large in Welsh ferrous industries. Yarranton allegedly did turn out some trial batches somewhere in Worcestershire in 1665, but although he claimed technical success, he presumably failed to compete with the imported product (a problem not unfamiliar to us today!). It is not known whether his efforts infringed Dudley and Chamberlayne's patents, but being both a Parliamentarian and a Presbyterian, must have made him seriously unpopular with such staunch Loyalists. In fact they may have maintained the patent just to thwart a dastardly Roundhead Republican. Actually Yarranton's authorship of pamphlets such as *How to pay debts without money*, and *How to outdo the Dutch without fighting*, made his bona fides slightly questionable.

In any case the mid 1660s was not the time to be setting up this sort of business. The metallurgical trades were in the doldrums and prices for iron products including tinplate were being slashed.

Nothing further seems to have happened in Britain until the metals boom of the 1690s. Everyone wanted to get into iron, copper, lead etc, but despite several patents being issued for the tinning of sheet iron, no one seemed to want to challenge the Continental tinplaters. There is anecdotal account of a works being set up at Bisham, near Windsor for making *'Iron plates tynned over'* around 1700, but there is no evidence that it worked for long, if at all. In any case the problems of a newcomer breaking into a mature industry would have been considerable. Apart from patent rights and commercial considerations, there were technical difficulties, not in the comparatively simple coating process of tinning, but in the production of the iron plates. These could only be made by using a tilt hammer, a fearsome apparatus where a massive mandrel carrying (usually) 4 cams was rotated by a water wheel at around 20 r.p.m. These cams depressed the helve of a hinged hammer raising its perhaps 200 Kg head and allowing it to fall thunderously onto an anvil, beating a skilfully manipulated iron bar into a flattish sheet, which was then doubled and re-doubled into a pack and reheated and re-hammered until the individual sheets were approximately the desired thickness. A huge hunk of iron crashing down onto another hunk of iron some 80 times per minute must have made forgemasters very undesirable neighbours.

At this time Capel Hanbury, a Kidderminster

ironmaster was working a forge at Pontymoel, near Pontypool. When this forge had been established in 1425, it would have drawn its iron from bloomeries, which produced tiny blooms of questionable quality but by Capel Hanbury's time forges were using pig iron turned out by the blast furnaces that had been introduced in the mid 16th century. There were many similar forges in a vast swathe stretching from the west Midlands into Monmouthshire, using the rivers to power the trip-hammers and the trees from the steep valley sides to heat the furnaces. Some of these forges had their own blast furnaces, but others like Hanbury, drew their cast pigs from neighbouring iron works. The forges melted pig iron with charcoal in an air blast in a finery to oxidise the carbon into slag and produce a rough lump of wrought iron that would be beaten under the trip hammer for several hours to form a bloom. This bloom was then reheated in a chafery furnace again using charcoal and then hammered into a bar of tough, ductile wrought iron. This seemingly roundabout blast furnace/pig iron route of making wrought iron gave a far better product and could be done on a scale far outside the scope of the old bloomeries. This charcoal method held sway for producing wrought iron until the early 19th century when puddling furnaces enabled coke to be used.

Most forges produced iron for the blacksmiths or for the various emerging Midlands industries, or as modern forges do, shaped forgings as finished or semi-finished products. Hanbury concentrated on a niche market producing iron for the wire makers that flourished along the river Wye turning out wire for the woollen industry.

This wire was used in Fulling Cards, the wire brushes used for untangling the fleeces prior to spinning the wool.

By the end of the 17th century Hanbury and his son John were also producing 'Japan' ware - domestic articles fabricated from iron plate and coated with a baked-on finishes in emulation of an ancient Japanese technique. By this process now associated with trashy trays, biscuit tins and such, the Hanburys made vessels and tableware of great beauty. They were by no means cheap, but with the cost of silver and pewter rising, these products found a ready market. This 'Pontypool' ware (now much collected) demanded a substrate that was smoother and of more consistent gauge than could be readily produced by hammer. Since rollers were used by his wire-making customers, it was natural that he should look to rolling for producing his sheet. Rolling, or *'Squeezing between cylinders'*, besides being well established for producing the narrow strip used for wire, was also used to produce lead sheet to an even, pre-determined thickness for roofing and drainage possibly even before Leonardo da Vinci had allegedly 'invented' the technique. Rolling iron, even hot iron, in appreciable widths was a different matter, but Hanbury was able to show that with multiple passes between water-powered rollers, whose gap was progressively reduced by means of wedges, iron sheet of unprecedented flatness could be turned out twenty times faster than hammering.

Whilst water-powered trip hammers carried on producing forgings for more than two centuries, over the next decades rollers displaced them for sheet production.

Whereas a trip hammer could be built by the village blacksmith and carpenter, mill rollers and stands called for specialist foundries. Thus what had been a rural craft began to need an industrial infrastructure.

It seems that the Hanburys were rolling iron sheet for their Pontypool Ware in the 1690s but it is not clear when they went in for the production of tinplate as we know it. Brooke, normally regarded as reliable in such matters, suggests that Capel did so in 1665 with Yarraton's assistance, but it is more probable that production, or at least serious production, commenced much later possibly by John after his father's death in 1704 following the 1706 increase in import duty on tinplate.

Although precise dates conflict, Hanbury and Pontypool's claim to the first British commercial production of tinplate is unchallenged.

When the Hanburys went in for tinplate manufacture may be in doubt, but why is less obscure. In 1670 the London wireworkers had been granted a Royal Charter *that* gave them exclusive rights, to work and sell wire products within the *'Cities of London, Westminster and Southwark and five miles compass thereof'*. In order to make numbers up to an appropriate level, the tinsmiths were lumped in with them, they being given similar exclusivity to work *Tynned Plate'*, and to sell their wares in the same area, their craft being defined as; *The Trade Arte and Mistery of Tynne Plate Workers als Wyer Workers of the City of London*. This *Worshipful Company*, an offshoot of the august *'Honourable Crafte and Fellosship of Fraunchised Men of Ironmonger'*. Although they were not admitted as a full City Livery Company until 1776, the Charter allowed them to demand a 7-year apprenticeship for full membership and authorised them to set the minimum prices that their members were allowed to charge on an extensive list that included; apple roasters, basters, boilers, boxes for everything from candles to snuff, canisters, upright kettles, fish kettles, pastry pans, dripping pans, porringers, shovels, speaking trumpets, cheese toasters and pots of every kind including pots to spit in! Planished pieces (hammered, double curvature items as opposed to the cut, bent and soldered products) included spoons, chocolate pots and strainers for oranges.

Although the Guilds Armorial Rights were not granted until 1957, their arms appear in stained glass windows in their own city church of St. Margaret Lothbury, Guildford Cathedral, the Guildhall Crypt as well as the respective Halls of their associated Guilds, the Ironmongers and the Tallow Chandlers. Through this Worshipful Company, the Hanburys being closely involved with the wire trade would have been in touch with the tin workers and have been aware of their growing dissatisfaction with both the quality and the duty-inflated price of the imported plate and their frustration that their petition to Queen Anne to abate the import duty, had been dismissed. The business opportunity that this offered would surely not have escaped such astute businessmen as the Hanburys.

2

From Experiment to Industry

By the mid 18th century British tinplate was beginning to be taken seriously so it was unsurprising that potential competitors wanted to know about it. In 1753 & 1755 a Swede, R. R. Angerstein made two journeys to see and report on the state of British industry. Fortunately his notes survive and have been published.

During his progress though Monmouthshire he described the process –

The tinbar is heated eight times before rolling is completed – after the initial reheating it is passed eight times between the rollers which are screwed down a little between each pass.

Angerstein explained how the plate was doubled twice during the course of the heating and rolling and how the four-thick pack was sheared into two so that a bar produced eight sheets. He also described the manufacture of the rolls, cast from re-melted iron scrap, (Considered to produce a more stable casting than virgin pig-iron), the roll-neck being turned between centres on a lathe, but the working face of the roll was apparently turned in-situ in the actual roll stand. –

By means of a square piece of steel, the edge of which is forced against the roll by a wedge.

This would have called for considerable skill since a roll had (and still has) to be finished fractionally concave since when hot the diameter at the centre increases very slightly more than at the ends. One must assume that the rolls must have then been less hard than modern rolls since until the introduction of Cubic Boron Nitride tooling in the 1980s, rolls (or at least work rolls) could only be serviced by grinding. The turning could not have been a quick process and whilst refurbishment would not have taken the *four or five days* Angerstein describes as necessary for a new roll to be *finished to perfection*, a considerable interruption to production is inferred.

Angerstein described the rolls as being 11" diameter and 14" long (working face?) with necks 7½" diameter, apparently bought in an'as cast' condition, the carriage from Bristol adding considerably to the cost.

He described how one end of a roll was formed into a 4' square section and was coupled to a similarly square-ended drive shaft by a sleeve with a square bore, very similar to the present-day system. It is interesting that the bearings by which the rolls were located and pressed together were called chocks, just as their modern equivalent are today. Each chock was positioned on two posts having their upper ends threaded to carry nuts that by means of a spanner could progressively force the rolls together. This screw mechanism was actually invented by Capel Hanbury's son John. It replaced the use of wedges and was still in use 200 years later, not differing in principle from the modern electrically driven screw jack. A recess in the chock accommodated a segment of what Angerstein calls *non-ferrous* metal, presumably a bronze or brass insert, also in use until displaced by roller bearings in the strip-mill era. Interestingly he showed both the upper and the lower rollers being driven by separate water wheels – a complex and unnecessary arrangement that certainly did not persist.

By the late 18th century, the pattern of producing the sheet that would last for almost two centuries had been established – the pack mill process. The basic unit being the mill, comprising a pair of stands one with roughing rolls the other with finishing rolls. New or newly refurbished rolls would be used in the finishing stand which when part worn, would be removed and re-installed in the roughing stand. There was a pair of furnaces with each mill, one for heating one for re-heating. There would also be a doubling squeezer and a crocodile shears, driven from the mill drive shaft.

A mill at that time had a crew of three, a Rollerman, a Furnaceman and a Behinder, there being then no Doubler, since the frequent breaks taken to allow the rolls to cool, gave the Roller man and the Behinder an opportunity to double and shear work in hand. The team appears to have shared around £1 (£125 or so in today's money); per week The Rollerman would have got almost half of this, with the Furnaceman not far behind, leaving little for the Behinder. Even so the latter's pay and the similar sums received by other workers were riches indeed compared with agricultural wages. Forge workers seem to have done even better with the three men per hammer sharing almost £2 per week, and the top blast furnace-men possibly doing better still.

Skilled metal workers had a double edge in the labour

market at this time. Firstly manipulating metal was regarded as an arcane, almost infernal art, blacksmiths being regarded more as professional men than tradesmen, secondly they were in an emergent and expanding technology where demand was outrunning skills-supply, invariably a lucrative situation. Even lesser skilled men such as nail-makers, could take home 15/- (75p) per week on piecework. A ploughman, the top man in agriculture, might get a free house but his cash-in-hand could be little more than 1/- (5p) per week.

The plates having been hot-rolled and sheared to size, were annealed and scraped to remove scale, then (in more recent times), cold-rolled before being soaked in 'lees' (Bran water) and scoured with sand.

The ensuing tinning process then consisted of three dips, the first into a very hot tin 'pot', followed by a dip into a pot at a lower temperature to give lustre, and finally just the bottom inch or so was dipped into a very hot pot to remove the tin that had run down and clung in a bead to the lower edge of the plate. Each pot had a layer of tallow floating on the molten tin to act as a flux.

After tinning the plates were hand cleaned with bran and a pad of cotton tow before being boxed. A typical box contained 225 plates 10½" x 13½", a mill crew being expected to make 3 boxes per day. Despite modern boxes being twice this size, latter-day pack mills produced up to 50 times as many. Tin consumption was stated to be 14lb per box (or 30lb in modern box terms) as against not much more than 1lb per box at the end of the pack mill era.

John Hanbury having died in 1834, it would have been his son, another Capel that Angerstein met. He had expanded the tinplate business, having two sets of rolls for tinplate and one for *Large Black Sheets;* this latter mill had rolls a massive 26" long and up to 13" in diameter. Angerstein describes how he employed the two Allgood brothers to make, lacquer and decorate items from these latter sheets. It must have been reasonably profitable, to say the least, 1/6 (7.5p) to 2/- (10p) being instanced for snuffboxes and 8/- (40p) to 18/- (90p) for tea trays. This tea tray figure converts on a Price Index basis to well over £100 in present day money and to an eye-popping near £1000 in wage-rate terms. Clearly Hanbury's Pontypool Ware was catering for the 'Carriage Trade', a notch above the very slightly more modest tinplate market.

After Capel's time the whole works went into decline no doubt hastened by the opening of tinplate and sheet works in Worcestershire, Staffordshire, Yorkshire and Somerset. Fortunately things were revived at the end of the century by a descendant, (yet another Capel) who had assumed the surname of Hanbury Leigh. Under his guidance, Pontypool as a two-site works (Central and Osborne) grew to a 10-mill concern, eventually accounting for almost half of the total capacity of the Partridge, Jones and John Paton combine that came to dominate Monmouthshire's tinplate production.

Following Pontypool's pioneering venture into tinning, it was the mid 1700s before there were further developments in Monmouthshire, Ponthir near Newport opening in 1747 and Caerleon a few years later. Ponthir was a 2-mill plant built by Jenkins and Conway, descendants of these partners remaining in possession right up to its 1890s closure. The early history of Caerleon is obscure, it is said to have been a forge purchased by Messrs Griffiths and Watkins in 1749 who shortly afterwards commenced tinning. It passed through a number of hands before ending up in the hands of Partridge, Jones and John Paton. It was a 4-mill works but not all its mills were exclusively devoted to tinplate. Just over the border into Gloucestershire were the two Lydbrook forges, leased by Richard Reynolds, later associated with Carmarthen Tinplate works, and the John Partridges, father and son, where anecdotally tinning commenced in 1760 although it is unlikely that any tinning was done until 1806, by which time T. Allaway had replaced Reynolds and had erected a 2-mill plant. They traded as Partridge and Allaway until selling out to Richard Thomas in 1872, who expanded the plant to 5 mills.

Not far away at Redbrook, Reynolds and the Partridges also leased a forge, where there had been industrial activity from at least the 15th century. It had a landing point on the Wye and from 1812 was served by the Monmouth and Coleford Tramway, (Obviating slow and costly pack mules and donkey trains). On part of an adjacent copper works site Townsend and Wood erected a tinplate works in 1771. By 1796 they were shipping out of Chepstow 43 tons of tinplate annually. There is a report of 1798 stating that there were two mills with rolls 14" diameter and 18" long and that one was steam driven and the other water-powered. If this is correct it would be one of, if not the, earliest example of steam in the tinplate industry. This works eventually became a 3-mill plant under the Redbrook Tinplate Company flag.

All these plants must yield precedence to Kidwelly in Carmarthenshire where forging was begun in 1719 and tinning not long after and justly claims to have been the second works in Britain to do so. For much of that century its fortunes under the Morgan family were intertwined with the Carmarthen Iron Works. Kidwelli was however not a significant producer until the 19th century when rebuilt by Haselwood, Hathaway & Perkins, it became a 7-mill establishment.

Glamorganshire came into the picture when the then century-old Ynyspenllwch forge at Clydach in the Swansea Valley was taken by John Morris and Thomas Lewis in 1741. Here the rolling of wire had been carried out since at least 1726, and it would seem that they began rolling and coating tinplate in 1747 when Roland Pytt the owner of the Lydney forge joined them and one assumes made some investment. Their ground landlord Sir Humphrey Mackworth the Neath industrialist and builder of Gnoll House was a friend of the Hanburys so he may well have at least nudged his tenants towards this up and coming product although they did not 'Give up the day job', continuing to roll hoop and rod iron.

Around 1770 John Miers a London importer of German tinplate appeared on the scene, buying Ynyspenllwch presumably to try to safeguard supplies in the wake of the interruptions of the Seven Years War. Miers was from a distinguished Quaker family, an ancestor having been incarcerated during the

Commonwealth for refusing to take his hat off in a Cromwellian court. He however suffered serious opprobrium by abandoning the Quaker faith in favour of the Church of England. He was a most influential man in the tinplate trade, in 1752 following his father as Master of the Worshipful Company Wire & Tinplate workers, (200 years later a most distinguished descendant, Rear Admiral Sir Anthony Miers, VC, KBE, CB, DSO, would occupy the same office). There is record of John Miers chairing a meeting of the Tinplate Guild at the George and Vulture tavern, Cornhill in 1780 to set the price of tinplate for the whole of England and Wales. Among those present were Bristol industrialists James Harford and James Gatley who had interests in Melingriffith works.

John Miers does not seem to have moved to Wales but his sons John and Nathaniel did, the latter's son John Nathaniel marrying into the great Hill family of Penydarren iron works, who sponsored Trevethick's pioneering locomotive, a cousin, Mary married into the Hanbury family of Pontypool. John Nathaniel, who eventually served as High Sheriff of Glamorgan, carried on Ynyspenllwch in partnership with his cousin Samuel Fothergill Letterson.

In the meantime, over in the Neath valley at the Dulais Falls was a much prized industrial site, one of several in the Neath and Swansea valleys where hanging valleys caused by river capture created cataracts ideal for water power. A copper works had displaced a flour mill in 1588, in its turn replaced around 1667 by an iron forge, which in 1750 was leased to the same Pytt and Morris by the landlord John Llewellyn. Shortly afterwards the pair leased land on the river Neath at Ynys-y-gerwn where they started a tinplate works, drawing iron from the Dulais forge. By 1771 Pytt had been succeeded by his son-in-law, William Coles, and he and Lewis were bought out by John Miers leaving him in possession of the tinplate works, the Aberdulais forge and the Afon forge in the Aberavon hinterland to which was added in 1785 the Dulais New Forge. All these in due course devolved to the Miers/Letterson partnership. The family fortunes were in no way harmed by John Nanthaniel's sister Molly marrying Sir Robert Mackworth, who numbered both tinplate works amongst his land holdings. Married aged 16, Molly was widowed at 18 but married secondly Capel Hanbury Leigh thus further strengthening the interweaving of the dynasties.

Ynys-y-gerwn was described in 1798 by the Rev. Richard Warner. –

A little further on, an artificial curiosity afforded us amusement – the tinplate works at Ynysygerwen. Here with astonishment the operation of machines of which we had no idea; rollers of such immense power as reduced bars of iron two inches thick to the thickness of a crown piece by passing them a certain number of times through their revolving cylinders; and sissars [Scissors] cutting bars in sunder of half an inch thick with the same ease that a fair seamstress would divide a wristband. When by the repeated pressures of the rollers, the plate is reduced to a sufficient thinness to receive a coating of tin it is cut by the sissars into sheets of a proper size. These are scoured well with sand and immersed in an acid liquor where they are suffered to remain for some time, and then quickly and perfectly dried, a process pursued in order to clear them of every speck of rust, the smallest particle of which would prevent the tin from adhering to the iron as no metal will combine itself with any earth, and rust is nothing more than the earth of iron.

The plates thus cleaned are next plunged vertically into a pot containing melted tin, the surface of which with pitch suet or some fatty substance to prevent the calcinations of the tin and to make the surface of the iron more inclined to receive its coating. By this immersion the tin adheres itself immediately to the plates and they are taken out completely tinned, being afterwards well rubbed with bran in order to give them a more brilliant appearance. They are packed in chests and sent to Neath to be shipped for the London, Liverpool or Bristol markets.

(This is a very early instance of acid rather than lees or sour rye being used to pickle the plates, a practice that did not become universal until well into the 19th century).

By 1810 there were difficulties. Lettsom wanted to expand, Miers counselled caution, understandable in the then wartime conditions, so they split up with Miers retaining Ynyspenllwch, trading as J. N. Miers & Co while Lettsom trading as John Miers & Co. ran Ynys-y-gerwn and the Aberdulais and Afon. Whilst the Afon forge was a little remote, forged bars could be readily taken from Aberdulais up the Neath river to Ynys-y-gerwn by a weir and cut off the river.

After J.N. Miers death in 1814 Ynyspenllwch, then

having besides the rolling mills, fineries, forges and two blast furnaces, was taken on in 1825 by William Llewellyn and John Cook. By the mid-19th century it was in the hands of Henry Strick who was later to become a prominent proprietor and was a relative by marriage of Percy Player who became 'Mr Clydach'. Now almost forgotten, Ynyspenllwch became a modestly important 5-mill establishment, historically notable in that it was the first works in an area that would become the centre of gravity of Welsh tinplate manufacture, also when it was taken by Mr Richard Thomas in 1867, he and others including W.Gethin floated it as the Ynyspenklwch (sic) Iron and Tinplate Company Limited, probably the earliest limited company in the tinplate industry. Curiously, when Thomas left in 1875, he took over Lydney tinplate works, built on the site of the ex-Pytt forge).

Bankrolled by his Attorney General father-in-law, Sir William Garrow, Letterson erected blast furnaces and rolling mills at Cwmafon, but by 1823 his spending became too much for even the long-pursed Sir William. Bereft of his backer Letterson fled abroad and the whole including Ynysygerwen, the forges and the part-built Cwmafon works was taken over by his manager John Vigurs, who although backed by a Mr Leonard Smith, Vigurs ability to purchase the concern suggests that he had prospered better than his boss! Around 1830 Vigurs closed down Ynysygerwn and moved the tinning equipment and workforce to the new Cwmafon site. This Cwmafon complex became the 9-mill Copper Miners tinplate works.

The Miers family, despite severing connection with industry remained leading members of the Neath and Swansea valleys communities into the 20th century, but the sole local reminder is Miers Street in Swansea that commemorates the building of the district in the 1850s on Miers land derived via the Mackworth connection. Nationally the Miers continue to excel in such disparate fields as the Army, Diplomacy and Fine Arts.

The mid 18th century saw developments in east Glamorganshire. Melingriffith forge on the banks of the river Taff, just north of Cardiff occupied the site of a 17th century ironworks that had in turn usurped the site of a very ancient corn mill. The forge drew its iron from Pentyrch Ironworks (reputedly having the first blast furnace in Wales), ideally sited up-river close to iron ore, limestone, trees and water-power. Melingriffith's owners were Bristol men described as 'Adventurers', not in the modern pejorative sense, but because they 'Ventured', although in those days of unlimited liability, they risked the 'Adventure' of losing their shirts if their affairs went sour. Indeed at the end of the Seven Years War in 1763 they were faced with such a possibility to the loss of orders for iron cannon, then their ironworks' main product. Consequently they decided to diversify and erected a 2-mill tinplate works at the forge site. Quite how successful they were is not known, they certainly faced some problems since the ironstone from the Garth mine adjoining the Pentyrch works produced iron that was too phosphoric for tinplate use, so that for tinplate orders Pentyrch had to add Lancashire and Forest of Dean ores to the smelt. This may have contributed to their decision in 1768 to sell out to Bristol iron merchants Reynolds Getley & Co, who combined the Melingriffith forge and ironworks with the Pentyrch works. Like so many entrepreneurs they were also Quakers, but by 1786 they had dropped out and the Partridges having come in, they were joined by Harford, another Bristol Quaker who together owned mines in Cornwall and had interests in the American colonies. The latter had enabled them to obtain iron from Maryland and Virginia where both charcoal and labour were cheaper, but the American war of Independence had seriously interrupted supplies. They did have access to Russian iron but again war with the French interrupted supplies. Consequently forges and ironworks such as those at Machen and Bassaleg were taken over.

Before the end of the century, puddling was being done at Pentyrch with tinbar iron being supplied to Miers' Ynyspenllwch works as well as to Melingriffith, the latter no longer reached by packhorses but by tub boats on the river Taff via a feeder cut to a lock at Radyr Weir. In 1815 the tub boats were replaced by a tramway along the West bank of the river, by which time Reynolds still retained an interest but John Partridge had dropped out, his place being taken by his nephew Richard Blakemore, backed by Bristolian R J Tomlinson and T. Pritchard of Ross. Most of these partners had interests in other iron works and forges as well as having merchanting connections with Bristol, so were quite a powerful team, with the 12-mill tinworks being described as the largest in the country and incidentally a pioneer in the provision of workers' housing.

Some years later Melingriffith found itself in a lot of bother when the Glamorganshire Canal was found to be a handy source of water. The canal people were not best pleased at the prospect of water that should have been floating their boats, driving the rolls at Melingriffith. The river-driven pump that the works was forced to install to replenish the canal has been restored.

Size apart, Melingriffith was important technically. An employee, Thomas Morgan is credited with the invention of the 'Crocodile' shears, with the use of sulphuric acid for pickling and with annealing in sealed boxes. After a succession of local owners it was taken on in 1882 by James Spencer who had been the firm's sales agent in Liverpool, a further example of backward integration. Six years later it was in the hands of Richard Thomas, by now a tinplate tycoon. In 1893 this works achieved widespread fame as the developers of the eponymous tinning pot, that enabled tin thicknesses to be dramatically reduced, a timely contribution to the industry during the lean post-McKinley decade.

In or around the 1760s Robert Morgan the proprietor of Kidwelly works, set up a 2-mill tinning department at his Carmarthen forge and furnace, which was one of the many ironworks erected in the 17th and 18th centuries to meet the increasing demand for iron, particularly for an increasingly sophisticated agriculture. The Carmarthen works still being an iron works would seem to make it the first 'integrated' works converting iron ore into finished tinplate on the one site.

Iron masters were unpopular for many reasons. Like other industrialists, they tended to buy up flourmills as a source of power, causing problems at a time of increasing populations, and they could pay much above agricultural wages, upsetting rural economies. Most serious was their voracious demand for charcoal. Charcoal 'Colliers' would travel considerable distances into Breconshire and beyond, felling trees by the thousand, often without the landowner's knowledge, confident that an iron master would not 'Ask questions'.

Unlike a forge furnace, once a blast furnace had been fired up it could not be allowed to go out during the four or five month campaign, so that an ironmaster known to be short of charcoal would find the colliers sharply upping their prices. Charcoal was usually stored in secure, windowless warehouses – partly to avoid the contents being stolen and sold back, but also to prevent the colliers discovering that the stockpile was low. In the later 18th century smelting with coke gained ground, particularly since there were laws prohibiting the burning of hardwoods needed by the expanding navy. With an abundance of beech that was often not subject to prohibition, these local furnaces were slow to go over to coke particularly as coke-iron was not considered ductile enough for sheet-work.

At about this time the fourth county (Pembrokeshire) became involved in tinplate, albeit briefly, with the Penygored forge commencing tinning around 1770. This most improbably located works was at of all places, the Teifiside salmon fishing village of Llechryd This might be termed a 'Rogue' siting, presumably to be near a charcoal source. Initially it was started by Walter Lloyd of Coedmore, who had bought the Llechryd forge in the 1850s and after passing through several hands the tinplate works became the property of Sir Benjamin Hammett MP, Alderman of the City of London (Who was responsible for the ending of the burning of women at the stake for High Treason, a crime that included counterfeiting coinage). Sir Benjamin built a fine house, Castell Maldwyn right alongside the works. He clearly carried clout since in 1793; he obtained an Act of Parliament exempting him from paying duty on coal shipped into Cardigan for use in his works (Coal would have been used in the tinworks furnaces, if not in the forge).

Shortly after his death, his son took up residence and paid suit to a Cardigan lady, she somewhat understandably demanded that the works not only be closed, but also razed to the ground, before she would set foot in Castell Maldwyn. Since although Sir Benjamin had built a horse-towpath along the Teifi as far as Cilgerran, the rest of the trip to Cardigan had to be expensively man-hauled, so carriage costs would have been heavy. Thus his gallant gesture to shut up shop was probably occasioned by business necessity rather than conjugal ambition.

It is difficult to extimate the size of the works, one account describes it as immense yet the tinplate output suggests at most two mills, 200 or even 300 men are spoken of but such large figures are suspect. Part of the works site subsequently formed the foundations of a substantial and still extant stable block. The canal that supplied the water wheels is still traceable.

The 18th century list was completed by the Tydu iron forge that occupied the site of an early copper works at Rogerstone near Newport, being extended in 1790 to include tinplating. Despite the all-pervading grasp of the Partridge, Jones combine, it remained a staunchly independent 2-mill works.

If one stretches the 18th century to include 1800, then one may in fact include a fifth south Wales county, Breconshire, with the opening that year of a single-mill plant at Gilwern near Abergavenny that despite its small size survived until 1880. Like many tinplate works geographically tied to iron works, the switch to steel substrate killed it.

However for the time being iron ruled the tinplate roost. Notably not from the big ironworks that stretched in a great arc along the northern rim of the south Wales coalfield – they were again busy with munitions of war to fight the French. Iron for tin plate was the product of the forges fed from the smaller more marginal blast furnaces.

3

The Great 19th Century Leap Forward

The early 1800s brought the food can, a world-changing invention that would make the 19th century the century of tinplate.

In 1795 the Frenchman Appert had shown that food heated and sealed in a container would keep fresh indefinitely, and in 1809 he was awarded a 12,000 franc prize that Napoleon had offered for a practical means of victualling his armies that were then bestriding Europe. Appert used glass jars, heavy, fragile and comparatively costly, as also did Englishmen Bryan Donkin and John Hall, but in contrast Augustus de Heine and Peter Durand used tinplate containers and filed a patent in 1810. Their canisters were more akin to strongboxes than modern cans and called for the skill of a safebreaker to gain entry, but they unlocked the floodgates of demand for tinplate.

They sent a sample of 'Preserved Beef' to the Duke of Wellington who pronounced it excellent and recommended that the process be used for troops' rations. Regrettably, 19th century military contractors being what they were, the quality of the meat in the containers initially supplied to the Army and Navy fell somewhat short of the sample

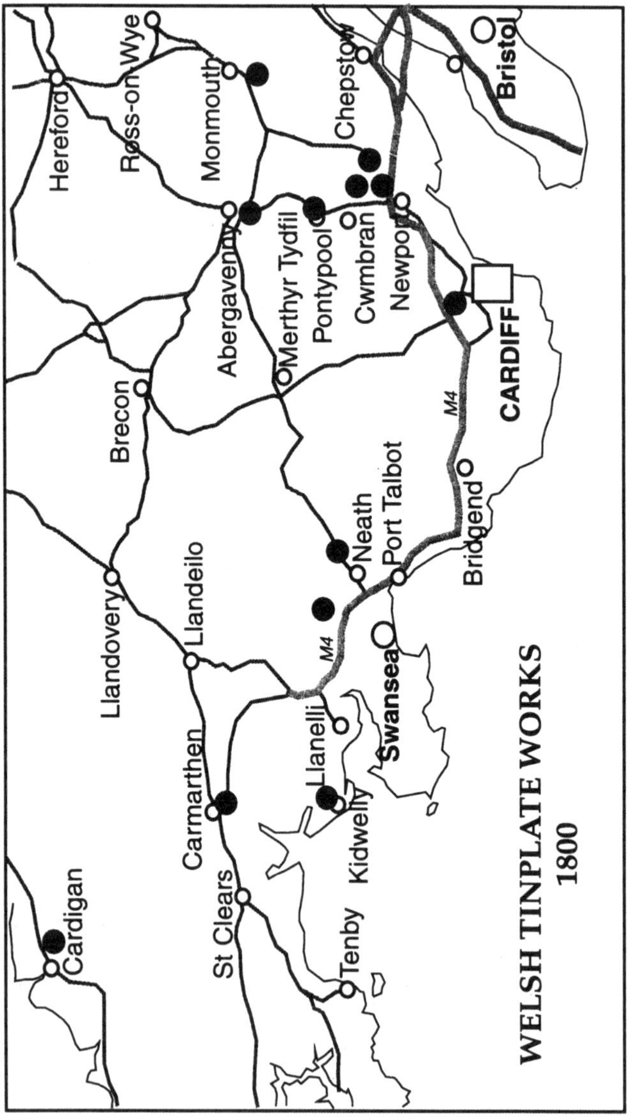
WELSH TINPLATE WORKS
1800
Hereford
Ross-on-Wye
Monmouth
Chepstow
Bristol
Abergavenny
Merthyr Tydfil
Pontypool
Cwmbran
Newport
CARDIFF
Brecon
M4
Port Talbot
Neath
Bridgend
Llandeilo
Llandovery
Swansea
M4
Llanelli
Carmarthen
Kidwelly
St Clears
Cardigan
Tenby

sent to his Grace, and it is said that its consumption called for greater heroism that facing the Republican Guard.

Eventually the contents would improve and Havelock's men would relieve Lucknow can-victualled and Kitchener's men would march on Khartoum no longer having to wrestle with rancid camel-flesh and Britannia's wave-ruling seamen would no long have to fight scurvy with limes. Travellers would enjoy fresh food, administrators of the outposts of Empire would no longer have to subsist on fish, fowl and fauna of doubtful provenance and stay-at-homes would be able to savour out of season and exotic comestibles.

In the meantime, by 1819 Ezra Dagget and Thomas Kensett were canning fish in New York and Charles Underwood was canning fruit and vegetables in Boston. In Britain exploration was all the rage and would be transformed by canned foodstuffs. The Parry, Franklyn and Belcher Arctic expeditions of 1824, 1845 and 1852 respectively would scarcely have been possible without canned goods.

In these early days, making the tins was a most 'labour-intensive' procedure. The rectangles for the bodies could be sheared but until 1847 when stamping was introduced, the circles for the ends had to be cut out with tin-snips, 150 being the most that even the best craftsman could turn out in a 12-hour day. The factory-made cans were sent to the canners complete with both ends in place, with just a comparatively small hole left in the lid, thus the contents needed to be at least semi-fluid. Hence one of the first mass-market offerings in 1856 was Borden's canned milk. 1869 the lock-seaming machine enabled cans to be supplied open-topped, the canner fixing the lid after filling Eventually the development of automatic soldering enabled not only cylindrical cans but also the dedicated cans for corned beef, fish and so on, to be machine made.

Although almost all the can-making developments were American, America did not much take to canned food until the Civil War (1861-1865), when it fed both armies, making it the first conflict where troops did not have to 'Live off the land'.

The defining year for canned food was 1867 when the Armour brothers opened their meat packing plant at Chicago. Two years later the Heinz brothers set up shop and although initially their 57 varieties did not include canned goods, they most certainly would later. Other firms followed with plants in the USA and the Argentine, creating a huge demand for tinplate, largely supplied from south Wales.

Expansion was not purely American driven, with long-range steam ships not yet refrigerated it was Corned Beef from the Prairies and the Pampas that enabled Europeans to enjoy wholesome and affordable meat. In Britain Angus Watson had yet to make Skipper's Sardines the supper of choice in millions of serried terraced homes, but long before the century was out the other great Liverpool importer Pelling. Stanley & Co would by courtesy of Mr John West, transform salmon from an exotic game fish, the preserve of the privileged and of poachers, to the nation's Sunday treat with Californian peaches and Carnation milk almost obligatory 'afters'.

While the menfolk went to work their food in tinplate snap-tins and their tea in tinplate billy-cans, their wives baked in 'tins' while on the stove tinplate kettles and cooking pots simmered. Children got under their feet playing with their tinplate toys. The milkman carried tinplate churns, finding his way in the chill-dark winter mornings with a tinplate lamp.

Tinplate became as universal in the 19th century as plastic would be in the 20th. In 1800 under a thousand persons in south Wales were directly employed in tinplate manufacture, ninety years later payrolls totalled twenty-five times that number. And on the subject of payrolls, in many industries pay was handed out in reusable tinplate containers.

It was a century when the number of households in Britain more than doubled – each additional household requiring the usual quota of kettles, pots, pans, jugs, plates, strainers etc, often most easily and cheaply produced in tinplate.

In America and elsewhere, population increases were even greater, all clamouring for tinplate goods. At the end of the Civil War a collection of states found itself a nation and very much a nation on the move. Pioneers pushing west in covered wagons to make 'cities' in the prairies, establish ranches, set up railroad construction camps or mining settlements, needing cheap and lightweight artefacts of every kind – tinplate was ideal. For roofing, a thousand tinplate 'slates' would weigh a fraction of the real thing, easing carriage and calling for less timbering. Dairy farmers were big users of pans, cans and vessels of every kind as well as coolers and separators, all in tinplate.

The 19th was also the century when waterpower yielded to steam, when coke displaced charcoal for iron making, and iron itself was overtaken by steel, but despite these improvements, production methods well established at the beginning of the century remained substantially unchanged 150 years later, when pack mill working ceased. Nevertheless there were technical developments, the idea having mills in tandem, had been patented in the late 18th century as had the idea of eliminating passing the pack over the mill stand by reversing the mills direction of rotation. This latter idea involved driving a mill roll by a chain wound around either end, a beam engine could then pull each chain in turn, thus imparting alternating rotation to the roll. This was a no-no notion, but Naismith's reversing steam engine of 1853 was not, although it does not seem to have been used in the tinplate industry, despite the fact that steam engines with their ability to operate through drought and frost were displacing the water wheel, enabling multi-mill works to be built on almost any patch of flat ground. Another idea was the three-high mill of which there were several patents in the mid 19th century. These ideas involved having a driven middle roll with rolls above and below it, thus a bar or sheet could be put through above the driven roll and returned back beneath it.

The greatest idea was the 4-roll mill invented (or some say cribbed from the Swedes!) by Newton in Ystalyfera in 1863. To achieve the greatest reduction per pass requires comparatively small diameter rolls, yet the smaller the roll the less is the pressure that it can transmit without breaking and certainly the upper roll at least, needs to be as heavy as possible to create that pressure, hence the idea of having, large diameter, back-up rolls to press the smaller work rolls together. This, the basis of the modern cluster mill, relieves the work rolls of all bending moments, enabling them to be small and to be very hard without too much concern about the consequent brittleness, also since the big, heavy back-up rolls suffer little wear, most roll changes involve the lighter, more easily handled work-rolls. Despite its obvious merits, this system was not even seriously considered until the strip-mill era of the mid-20th century.

The process began by heating the tinbar, a bar of iron (later standardised at 15-20′ long x 9″ wide and 3/8″ to 7/8″ thick) and rolling it to a suitable thickness, then shearing it in half, then again rolling, folding and cropping, all with appropriate re-heating, to produce two packs each of eight sheets.

Manning comprised four (later six) men, led by the Rollerman, an experienced and well-paid man, responsible for taking the hot bars from the Furnaceman who was the second man of the team and passing the material though the rollers and keeping the bite (the roller gap) appropriately adjusted, by the big screw jacks at either end of the stands.

The Rollerman always had to fight the temptation to speed matters up by closing the bite, or delaying reheating. Either could result in stalling not only the offender's own mill but also all the others with which it shared drive, making him gravely unpopular with his fellow Rollermen. More seriously it could result in breaking a roll, calling for a roll-change that lost his colleagues precious output bonuses.

Breaking a roll often involved automatic dismissal, unfairly so since a roll could be excessively brittle if over-chilled in manufacture. There is an often-repeated account of a west Wales Rollerman who having broken a roll, burst into the office of the notoriously unforgiving manager to plead for his job. There he found the manager – in intimate congress with the boss's wife. Not only did the Rollerman keep his job but was regarded as unsackable for the rest of his career.

The Rollerman was assisted by the Behinder, who caught the plates as they passed through the rolls, and grasping them in his tongs passed them back over the stand back to the Rollerman. The Rollerman would then skid the sheets along the cast iron clad floor, either to the Furnaceman who was responsible for maintaining a constant supply of hot bars and reheated packs, or to the Doubler, who ranked third in the team, for doubling or cropping. Doubling consisted of combining tongs and boot to partially fold over the sheet, the folding being completed with the squeezer driven by a cam on the mill drive shaft. Later a Helper and a Second Helper augmented the basic four.

The heat was infernal, the fumes insufferable, the noise stupefying. Screaming-hot, jagged edged plates, arcing through the air on long tongs or skidding along the iron-surfaced floor, caused burns and crippling lacerations. The average age of death was 45 years.

Quite separate was the 'Cold End', where the packs

were split (separated) and the sheets pickled, (acid replacing barley meal liquor around 1805), annealed, cold-rolled, re-annealed, tinned, washed, greased, hand-cleaned, assorted and packed (the processes varied with time and place). Just as busy, but with less heat and less 'stife', much of the work was also lighter and was where young boys, older or injured men as well as women were to be found.

In contrast to the Hot (or Mill End) where not a lot changed for 200 years, there were in the course of the 19th century a number of innovations to improve and part mechanise the cold processes.

Since each mill was virtually a self-contained unit, benefits of scale were limited and waterpower usually limited works to 2 or 3 mills. It was only the introduction of steam that gave larger works any appreciable advantage over smaller ones – hence the industry remained very fragmented. Even when the big combines emerged there was little amalgamation into larger production units.

The initial 19th century expansions took place in what was then Monmouthshire during wartime when metallurgical industries boomed and provided welcome employment at a time of agricultural hardship.

The first in the new century's works was Lower Pontnewydd, probably a single mill affair, started in 1802 by Messrs Conway and Jenkins. Drawings of cold mill rolls and standards furnished them by the Neath Abbey Iron Works in 1852 suggest upgrading. However the works, still under the Conway name, ceased in 1888, probably due to a combination of unsuitable siting and a lack of modernisation.

In 1806 there was a mention of 'Mr Crawshay's Tinplate works at Treforest, having a greater production than Melingriffith', already being described as 'the largest in the kingdom.' It is known that William Crawshay of Cyfarthfa works owned a forge at Newbridge, as Pontypridd was then called, but no evidence survives that tinplate was made there until the works was developed in 1836 by Crawshay's son, Francis. Admittedly it was quite an elaborate and integrated layout with 8 waterwheels, that included all aspects of iron making, but it never had more than 5 tinplate and 2 sheet mills. Iron making ceased there at the end of the 19th century but tinplate continued until WW2, under various ownerships until finally taken along with Melingriffith by Richard Thomas.

In 1807 the Conways opened the 2-mill Edlogan works at Pontrhydyrun in Monmouthshire. It was a much better proposition than Lower Pontnewydd and was expanded to 3 mills before being acquired by Richard Thomas in 1908.

In 1818 the Allways opened a tinplate works at Lydney where iron had been worked since at least the 13th century. This development on the site of the old Lower Forge was not of course actually in Wales but definitely part of the Monmouthshire/Forest of Dean industries arising out of the long-standing iron and wire working tradition. A port location and an early use of steam enabled this tinplate works to become an 11-mill establishment, by far the largest in the area one of only a dozen tinplate works to have more than 10 mills.

Furthermore having been taken over by Richard Thomas in 1884, it became the springboard for his domination of the tinplate trade in Wales and a major player in the world stage.

In 1826 the 2-mill Waterloo works was erected on the site of the Machen forge. It passed through several hands before closing in the 1870s. It was re-started in the 1890s expanded to 4 mills by Richard Thomas, and eventually taken over by Partridge, Jones & John Paton in 1920.

The Waterloo works was the last opening in Monmouthshire for almost two decades since tinplate was beginning its westward migration that started in 1822 with the opening of the Margam (Mansel) works. Like Lydney this was a dockside development, using an old forge as a basis, its 12 mills made it a larger works than Lydney but only about half of them were rolling plate for tinning. Initial proprietors were Reynolds and Smith who relocated many men from their Carmarthen works. Later trading as Robert B Byass this complex adjoining Guest, Keen and Baldwins Port Talbot and Margan steelworks, became part of Baldwin's in 1934. As has been mentioned the (eventually) 9-mill Cwmavon tinplate works was started in 1824 by Vigurs and Smith using plant removed from the Ynysygerwen works in the Neath valley. Smith having dropped out, Vigurs was joined by fellow Cornishmen Batten and James who diversified into copper smelting and famously ran a smoke tunnel up the western side of the valley to a chimney on the summit. In 1841 the resoundingly named 'Governors and Company of Copper Miners of England', took this works and the Pontrhydyfen Ironworks (whose unique stone acqueduct fed their water-wheels), as basis for their vast industrial enterprise that filled the Afon valley and were responsible for building much of the town of Cwmafon. Despite its domination for much of the mid-century the combine was dogged by financial troubles. They tried steel making during the 1890s but this was not a success. The 8-mill tin works, almost the last remnant of this bold enterprise closed during WW2.

In 1830 things edged further west again with the opening of the 4-mill (later 6-mill) Aberdulais tinplate works in the Neath valley by William Llewellyn on the site of the Dulais New Forge, one of the properties vacated by Vigurs on his move to Cwmafon.

It was later taken over by Joshua Williams with whom Gilbertson of Pontardawe would later be associated. In 1835, William Parsons came on the Swansea valley scene, opening a 3-mill water-powered tinplate works and forge on a branch of the canal at a cross roads some miles north of Swansea at a place subsequently known as Pontardawe. He also had the 2-mill Pheasant works on a basin of the canal at Trebanos. The Pheasant works proved ephemeral but the Pontardawe works did not.

Taken over in 1861 by William Gilbertson, who tiring of coping with financial problems not of his own making had resigned as manager of Cwmafon. Under the great Gilbertson dynasty Pontardawe became a multi-function steel and metallurgical complex that included 16 tinplate mills, 16 sheet mills and 6 Steel furnaces and would in due course diversify into high-duty steel for motor vehicles and incorporate the 6-mill Glanrhyd tinplate

Man-hauled barges on Teifi taking material from Penygored tinplate works c.1800

Holywell tinplate works, late 1860s
Courtesy Greenfield Valley Historic Society

South Wales tinplate works, Llanelli, c.1950
Courtesy Llanelli Library Service

R. T. Mills tinplate works, Llanelli, c.1950
Courtesy Llanelli Library Service

Clayton tinplate works, c.1956
Courtesy Trostre Works Cottage and Industrial Museum
Corus Packaging Plus, Llanelli

Remains of Old Castle tinplate works 2008
(Photo author)

Shearing 'Tinbars' to length. Clayton tinplate works, c.1955
Courtesy Trostre Works Cottage and Industrial Museum
Corus Packaging Plus, Llanelli

Heating 'Tinbars' prior to rolling. Clayton tinplate works, c.1955
Courtesy Trostre Works Cottage and Industrial Museum
Corus Packaging Plus, Llanelli

Rollerman and Behinder, Clayton works, c.1955
Courtesy Trostre Works Cottage and Industrial Museum
Corus Packaging Plus, Llanelli

Doubler. Clayton tinplate works, c.1955
Courtesy Trostre Works Cottage and Industrial Museum
Corus Packaging Plus, Llanelli

Rollerman. Drawing by the late Tony Evans
By kind permission of Mrs K Evans

Behinder. Drawing by the late Tony Evans
By kind permission of Mrs K Evans

Doubler squeezing. Clayton tinplate works c.1955
Courtesy Trostre Works Cottage and Industrial Museum
Corus Packaging Plus, Llanelli

Opening. Clayton tinplate works, c.1955
Courtesy Trostre Works Cottage and Industrial Museum
Corus Packaging Plus, Llanelli

Pickling girl. Clayton tinplate works, c.1955
Courtesy Trostre Works Cottage and Industrial Museum
Corus Packaging Plus, Llanelli

Washing machine. Clayton tinplate works. c.1955
Courtesy Trostre Works Cottage and Industrial Museum
Corus Packaging Plus, Llanelli

Washing. Clayton tinplate works, c.1955
Courtesy Trostre Works Cottage and Industrial Museum
Corus Packaging Plus, Llanelli

Cold Rolling. Clayton tinplate works, c.1955
Courtesy Trostre Works Cottage and Industrial Museum
Corus Packaging Plus, Llanelli

Polishing. Clayton tinplate works, c.1955
Courtesy Trostre Works Cottage and Industrial Museum
Corus Packaging Plus, Llanelli

Assorting. Drawing by the late Tony Evans
By kind permission of Mrs K Evans

Roll turning. Clayton tinplate works, c.1955
Courtesy Trostre Works Cottage and Industrial Museum
Corus Packaging Plus, Llanelli

Foden Hot Mill engine
Courtesy Kidwelly Industrial Museum.
(Photo Author)

Hot Mill stand
Courtesy Kidwelly Industrial Museum.
(Photo Author)

Screw-down and spanner
Courtesy Kidwelly Industrial Museum. (Photo Author)

Cold Mill engine and pulleys. Kidwelly tinplate works
Courtesy Kidwelly Industrial Museum. (Photo Author)

'Killer' roll adjusting spanner
Courtesy Trostre Works Cottage and Industrial Museum
Corus Packaging Plus, Llanelli. (Photo author)

Crocodile Shears
Courtesy Trostre Works Cottage and Industrial Museum
Corus Packaging Plus, Llanelli. (Photo author)

Millbrook Patent Rotary Pickling Machine
Courtesy Trostre Works Cottage and Industrial Museum
Corus Packaging Plus, Llanelli. (Photo author)

works. Steel making continued into the 1960s. Happily and almost uniquely, other metallurgical manufacture continues on the site.

The 1830s saw several works developed in the English Midlands, but only one other in Wales, the building (or rebuilding?) of the Treforest works.

The 1840s also saw a big surge of Welsh openings. In 1843 T & G Lewis started making tinplate on their Pontymister ironworks site. Successively owned by Banks & Co and Capt. P. S. Phillips who added a steelworks and formed the Pontymister Tinplate Company in 1880. Later it became the Monmouthshire Steel & Tin Plate Co and with 4 mills and 7 furnaces, the hub of the Partridge, Jones and John Paton empire. At about the same time as Pontymister started tinning, the great Ystalyfera Iron Company diversified into tinplate. Ystalyfera with its 11 blast furnaces, 42 puddling furnaces and numerous mills and forges, was a major force. Its output and its coal and ore requirements dominated the Swansea canal and its boss J.P.Budd dominated the Upper Swansea Valley. By 1885 iron was history as was the haulage of ore up the valley and the whole outfit, other than the 4-mill tinplate works closed, with the loss of hundreds of jobs, a blow from which Ystalyfera has never fully recovered.

In 1845 came two important openings that emphasise how, although the water wheel remained the basic power-source, the increasing use of steam was making the industry less river-dependent, encouraging coalfield sitings. The first was the 12-mill Abercarn Tinplate, again in Monmouthshire but very much in the south Wales Coalfield rather than in a sylvan vale. This works started by the Midlands firm of Biddulph and Spencer, was taken over by their manager Daniel Whitehouse, who ran it until 1895 when it was taken on by Richard Thomas personally, becoming part of Richard Thomas & Co in 1914 and finally closing in 1961. The second was the Upper Forest works at Morriston in the midst of the lower Swansea valley collieries. It started as a single mill, hijacking the site of an old flourmill, but rapidly grew having sheet mills furnaces and forges as well as 5 tinplate mills. John Jones Jenkins (later Lord Glantawe) a towering figure in Swansea industry came in briefly in 1858 but left the following year to start the adjacent Beaufort works. Unfortunately ten years later Hallam & Co. the then proprietors of Upper Forest became insolvent. The works was taken over by Whitehouse of Abercarn in 1872 but closed again shortly afterwards. It was re-opened merged with the Worcester works to form the great Upper Forest and Worcester works.

1846 saw another pair of openings Abertillery and Dafen. The former, like Abercarn, was coalfield located, but had the additional advantage of being close to an important foundry and a fine engineering company that lasted throughout the 20th century. The tinplate works passed through various hands until taken in 1914 by John Paton who held it up to his death in 1944, but although active until 1957, at one time having 10 mills, it was never part of the Combine co-founded by Paton.

The other development that year, Dafen had puddling furnaces and a steam hammer but was not massively important in the tinplate sense since its 5 mills were largely engaged in rolling black plate for galvanising and enamelling, an activity that outlasted its early 1930s cessation of tinning. Though only a minor tinplate works its importance lay in it being the progenitor of the 'Llanelli Phenomenon'. It was also notable in that the local sponsors were not backed by a landowner, an industrialist or a merchant, but by John Winkworth a dentist from Bath; emphasising the emergence of middle-class investors.

The Great Western (*neé* South Wales) Railway's arrival at west Wales in the early 1850s gave new siting possibilities and the new dock they built at Briton Ferry focused attention on that area, which was where the 4-mill Ferry tinplate works was opened in 1850 by David Morris, David Smith and Thomas Lister, it got into difficulties in 1882 along with the partners' other works, Gower, Old Lodge and Llangennech. Acquired eventually by Edgar Morgan it suffered a disastrous fire, re-opening again as the Vernon works, to again have problems in 1898 and be taken over by Percy Player of Clydach finishing up as part of the Briton Ferry group.

A year later J.S. Tregoning a Liverpool merchant and exporter originally from Cornwall, already associated with Llanelli Copper Works, opened the 2-mill (Later 5-mill) Llanelly Tinworks. This tinplate works, known later as the Morfa works, he ran in conjunction with the Cornish Bissoe Tin Smelting Company. This interesting combination assured Tregoning of supplies for his American exports, it gave Bissoe a guaranteed market for its tin and the works security of both tin supplies and sales. It was the first works in Llanelli primarily established to make tinplate and was well sited alongside the Dafen River and the Llanelli Railway. Tregoning later headquartered all three enterprises in Llanelli, where he became prominent in the towns public and civic affairs.

The same year the totally steam driven Landore works opened at Swansea. A number of works such as Aberdulais and Margam were using steam to back up water wheels but Landore seems to have been the first tinplate works to be totally steam dependant. In 1853 Richard Thomas' Lydney works had company when the nearby Parkend Forge opened a 2-mill tinplate plant that lasted until the industry's switch to steel hastened its 1881 closure.

The Crimean war brought a loss of business confidence that hit the tinplate trade. In 1850 tinplates were selling for around 27/- (£1.35) per box, before the end of that decade prices had fallen to around 24/- (£1.20p), yet tin had increased from under £80 per ton to over £130. Which with 8-9 lbs of tin being needed per box, added about 4/- (20p) per box on costs - effectively a 25% drop in revenue. This gave some impetus to Terne plate (Coating with a lead/tin alloy, usually 20% lead), acceptable for some uses but of course a big no-no, for food cans. It also gave rise to a remarkably rapid succession of patents for tinning equipment that enabled the thickness of the tin coating to be virtually halved, reducing per-box costs by around 2/- (10p).

In 1858 despite the pressure on profits, David Davies, a local entrepreneur, had the confidence to open the Cwmfelin works strategically sited alongside Bwrlais brook (for process water) and the South Wales Railway and the Brynhyfryd tramway that directly connected to the Swansea dock. At first a somewhat tentative 2-mill job it eventually ran to an exceptionally large 20 mills, with a steelworks, and an interest in several collieries, ultimately becoming the Jewel in the Crown of the Richard Thomas empire.

The 4-mill Cynon works was opened at Aberdare in the late 1850s as an offshoot of the Gadlys Iron works. Trading variously, with mixed success as Gadlys Uchaf Tin Plate Co, Smith & Davis, Hosgood & Smith, J.D.Lewis & Co, Dare Tinplate Co, Gadlys Tinplate, Aberdare Tinplate, Cynon Tinplate and Swansea Tinplate (in conjunction with Cwmfelin and the Lion works at Nantyglo), it clearly had more ups and downs than a fairground ride before enjoying relative stability when taken by Richard Thomas.

In 1859, as has been mentioned, John Jones Jenkins (Lord Glantawe) and several local worthies opened the Beaufort Tinworks on the site of the Lower Forest Copper works, previously one of the numerous forges powered by the river Tawe. They started with 2 mills, water driven with steam backup but their eventual 9 mills taken together with Cwmfelin and Upper Forest, emphasised the way that tinplate and other ferrous industries would replace copper as the basis of Swansea's industrial prosperity and that northern Swansea could almost equal Llanelli for tinplate manufacture. At the same time the Millbrook Works at Landore could match any as a centre of excellence for mill rolls, mill stands and similar heavy castings.

Swansea production was further augmented in 1863 by the Cwmbwrla Works. It had something of a false start since the proprietors, the Swansea Iron and Tinplate Co of Messer Bound and Voss failed in 1870. It was re-started two years later as the Swansea Tinplate Co, but real action came in the early 1880s when Morewood & Co of Llanelli took it on and integrated it by adding 2 Steel furnaces and a bar mill to its 8 tinplate mills. It became part of Richard Thomas' expanding portfolio in 1898.

1864 & 1866 saw developments in the Neath/Port Talbot area with the opening of the Avon Vale tinplate works at Port Talbot and the Melyn tinplate works at Melincryddan, Neath. The latter was started by Dr Robert Leach of Devizes who came to live at Vernon House at Briton Ferry, the managing director being Phillip Flower of Croydon whom he seems to have 'Head Hunted' from Robert Byass' Margam tinplate works. Flower was assisted and later succeeded by Robert Phillips who had managed the Briton Ferry Iron works. Thus this works was showing how industrialists were being drawn to south Wales and how ideas were being cross-fertilised through job changing. It is remarkable how in an era of a 'Job for life', senior men moved so freely from works to works. This movement was not confined to south Wales, since England, America and even Russia were 'In the loop'.

'The Melyn' was also notable for innovation. Leach patented an improved tinning pot and proposed that a number of rolls be placed in tandem (the basis of the strip mill) Flower had the then laughable idea of joining plates together into a long strip and winding it into a coil. It would be seventy years before this now so obvious way of working was adopted at Ebbw Vale. Melyn works in due course had 7 tinplate mills and 4 sheet mills, as well as open-hearth furnaces, with notable names such as Henry Eccles and J Percy Player on the board, eventually becoming part of the Briton Ferry Steel Company.

The Avon Vale Tinplate Company, later the Port Talbot Tinplate Company, a modest 3-mill outfit proved ephemeral but the same year another opening, the Hendy Works at Pontardulais did not. Although only a 3-mill undertaking, (later 4-mill) it adjoined both the Llanelly Railway and the Morlais colliery and it was the first of many works that would enable Pontardulais to claim to have more tinplate mills per thousand population than anywhere else in south Wales and probably indeed anywhere on earth. Hendy was another backward-integration being started in association with Edmund Boughton & Co, a Midlands based iron merchants, to safeguard supplies for the growing demand for tinplate in the Birmingham area. It was set up and managed by the redoubtable and splendidly named Octavius Williams who had started up the Morfa Works at Llanelli and would go on to found the Glamorgan works at Pontardulais.

With the gathering pace of openings, skilled labour was a problem, only solvable by poaching, Williams is believed to have enticed a number of men from both Dafen and Carmarthen works. Some jobs particularly in the Cold Roll and Tinhouse departments only called for limited skills, but an experienced Rollerman was worth his weight in tinplate and could almost write his own payslip, and of course the housing provided would have to be very much to his (and his wife's liking) before he would move jobs.

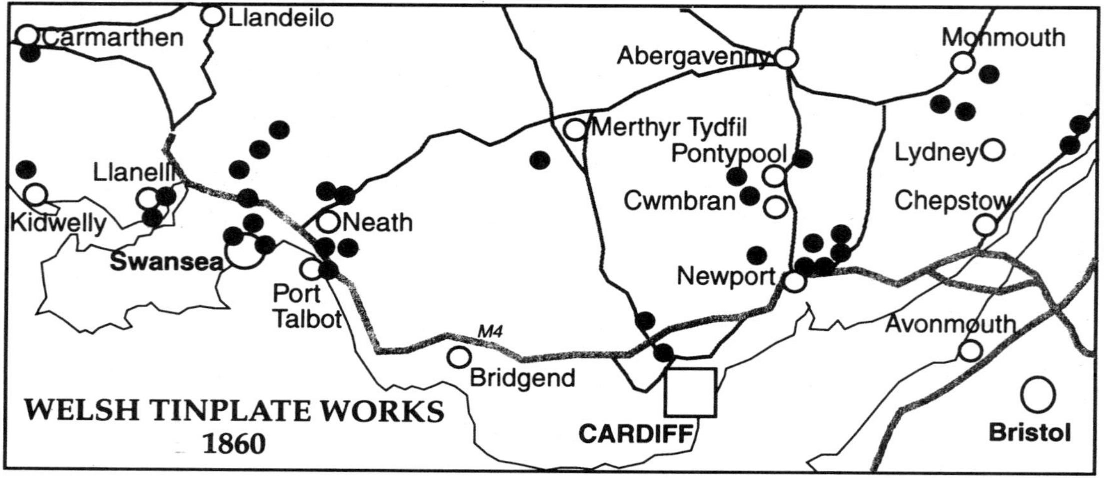

WELSH TINPLATE WORKS
1860

4

Llanelli and other phenomena

With steam and coal displacing trees and water, tinplate could escape the confines of remote valleys, proximity to the developing railway network and to collieries becoming the main siting imperative. Thus flat ground alongside a coalfield rail line was where new openings were taking place. Many formed the nuclei of towns such as Ammanford, Clydach, Garnant, Pontardawe and Pontardulais with the works proprietors contributing to the housing build but Llanelli could not only offer a ready-made township, (And a rorty and naughty one at that with innumerable pubs and allegedly more 'Actresses' than any other theatreless town in the country!) but also a port and an established tradition of metallurgical processing. Although by the time Llanelli came into the tinplate picture, water for power was of diminishing importance, but clean water for processing was certainly needed and it is said that the same water that made Llanelli's beer famous was the backbone of its tinplate industry. Like Swansea there were copper works, a valuable source of pickling acid, a fact that would eventually help to make the two towns the eventual lynch-pins of the industry.

In 1834 when Newport, Cardiff, Aberavon and so on were still fishing villages the Llanelly Railway & Dock Company, not only established rail communication with the hinterland collieries, but also created a 'floating' dock. This dock was the first in Wales with gates and a lock, a facility for which Swansea would have to wait nearly twenty years. The need to maintain the railway locomotives, the docks machinery and the winders of some of the earliest deep mines, led to the creation of a heavy engineering and foundry infrastructure that went on to serve tinplate works needs. The Margrave/Waddle partnership's Lanmore Iron Co. of 1836 was followed by the South Wales Iron Works, but Nevill's Foundry was probably the first to cater for tinplate works needs. These were followed by others such as the Llanelly Foundry & Engineering Company and the great Glanmor Foundry that became a leading maker of steel castings specialising in mill stands, rolls and other tinplate works machinery. When following their 1946 amalgamation, Richard Thomas & Baldwin decided to set up a centralised engineering facility, they took advantage of Llanelli's unparalleled accumulation of engineering skills to site it at Machynys.

Thus although Llanelli was in a sense a latecomer to tinplate with the first works in the district not opening until 1846 and the first in the town itself not established until 1863 not only did Llanelli end up with some eight or nine works, most were above average size aggregating to over 60 mills. In addition Pontardulais, Ammanford and the Amman valley being so well rail-connected, could be regarded as satellites of Llanelli, almost doubling this total of mills, making Llanelli the hub of much of the entire UK Tinplate industry.

The 1860s was a time of dramatic expansion for tinplate, a dozen being set up in south Wales alone during the second half of the 1860s. Llanelli's move into the big time started in 1863 when the 4-mill Marshfield works opened, sited unlike Dafen and Morfa on rivers, but right in the town where its sounds and smells mingled with that of the locomotives standing at the station, with Station Road a sea of people at change of shift. No way could anyone in the commercial part of the town be unaware that they were in a heavy-industrial community. Moreover it was not started as were so many, by carpet-bagging incomers but by established local figures led by Nevill a scion of the Birmingham button-making dynasty who had opened Llanelli copper works in 1804. Then they needed to secure supplies of brass for buttons (for the army to fight the French?). Now they needed to meet a demand for tinplate for the same purpose.

Old Castle followed in 1867 on a modest scale but at its 17-mill peak had an output almost unsurpassed by any other pack mill. It was on the site of the then disused Old Castle colliery, that took its name from an ancient British fort. It eventually became very much the senior partner in the Llanelli Associated Tinplate group. Significantly that same year C. W. Nevill (of Western works) had his own ship launched, this iron steamship, the *Naiad*, was built by The Iron Shipbuilding Company at a time when most Welsh built vessels were wooden sailing ships. This ship was intended to bring in copper from

Cornwall, the second Nevill ship, the *Llanelly* being dedicated to the carrying of tinplate to Liverpool and bringing back flour, sugar and indeed canned goods, to meet the burgeoning needs of Llanelli town. As the town's tinplate output grew with the American market dominating tinplate demand, these steamers became the nucleus of a fleet of ships, many Llanelli owned, shuttling to Liverpool, carrying boxes of tinplate for trans-shipment onto transatlantic vessels. In fact although by this time other ports were outstripping Llanelli's coal trade, tinplate more than made up the shortfall.

St David's (Yspitty) opened in 1869, on the site of an old copper works at a little industrial cluster that had grown up close to shipping points on the river Loughor, but which now had a new importance due to its proximity to the South Wales Railway. This was another venture by John Jones Jenkins the future Lord Glantawe, eventually having 10 mills, it was the first Llanelli works not to have its own forge and iron puddling furnace (Old Castle even also had its own ironworks), a wise and prescient choice since iron would soon be an irrelevance in the tinplate industry.

In 1872 the 5-mill South Wales Works was opened by Edmund Morewood, a Midlands galvaniser and his nephew J. H. Rogers. Morewood and Rogers were notable pioneers with numerous tinning and pickling patents and were the first to propose running rolls in tandem (the basis of modern strip reduction). South Wales was the first major enterprise on the marsh area that would eventually house most of Llanelli's heavy industry. Like most works they had to seek skilled labour wherever it could be found, and recruited one of their foreman from Merthyr Tydfil, then one of the great heavy industrial capitals of the world, he a Thomas Pugh eventually set up two of his sons in a retail business that grew into the famous department store, that with 'Morris the Realm' catered for the rising professional/managerial classes of the town. The South Wales Works was followed in 1876 by the adjacent Burry works, which at its peak was a mighty 16-mill enterprise.

Old Lodge opened in 1880 on the site of a comparatively modern (1852), but by now redundant ironworks. It was not a success at first but did better after 1889 when it was re-constituted as a 6-mill plant.

In 1890 the Ashburnham works opened, although very much a part of the Llanelli Phenomenon and latterly in the Llanelli Associated group, it was at Burry Port. This location was close to coal, railways and docks, offered the chance of a clear level site and access to new sources of labour. This 4-mill works was started by a syndicate headed by Lord Ashburnham, but was taken over by Thomas Bowen & Co of the Morriston tinplate works, and later run by Bowen's son-in-law A. A. Lewis.

The 1890s and early 1900s were not times to be in tinplate, but the trade generally was supported by galvanising particularly at Dafen, Gorse and Wellfield and by black plate for enamelled goods such as the song-famed 'Sospan fach', being made at specialised works such as Cambrian and later by the great Llanelly Stamping Company works, which was in 1911 itself one of the sponsors led by W. H. Edwards of Morriston, of the 4-mill Pemberton tinplate works.

Llanelli did not only supply the world with tinplate and tinplate goods, it also supplied the world with tinplate techniques In 1875 William Thomas of the Burry works went out to Russia with a number of men to set up tinplate making at Hughesovka, an ironworks town founded a few years earlier by John Hughes of Merthyr. Llanelli men founded tinplate works in Spain and in Italy, of course without Llanelli and other Welsh tin-men, there could scarcely have been an American tinplate industry at all.

Whilst Llanelli was developing, tinplate works were being established all over Wales, with 1867 seeing five new openings. Basil Jayne owner of the Clydach (Mon) Forge started a (2-mill?) works at Brynmawr in conjunction with the ubiquitous and soon to be ennobled J. J. Jenkins. Sited to be near a source of iron, it was very soon apparent that iron supplies would be irrelevant and the works closed within four years, Jayne transferring his tinplate interests to Hendy. The Rhiwderin Tinplate Company (*neé* Garth Iron & Tinplate Co) was started up near Newport as an offshoot of the Pontymister works, but it suffered and never really recovered from, the problems of the early 1880s, closing in 1887. Confusingly the totally unconnected Garth Sheet Iron Co opened the Llwydarth works near Maesteg in 1868. This innovative (later 5-mill) works, now almost forgotten, prospered in the 1890s under W. H. Edwards of Morriston (Daniel Edwards' son) who also ran the Dyffryn works.

Reverting to 1867 the spectacularly unsuccessful north Wales enterprise, Holywell Tinplate Works, was started in the Greenfield valley. That valley had been intensively industrialised to take advantage of the power of the Holywell stream, but by the mid 1860s the whole area was becoming marginalized by the advent of steam. Presumably the attraction was the pool of labour from the declining copper and other industries but closure came within three years.

Of more significance that year was the opening just outside Llanelli of the Llangennech works by a local man, Thomas Harris. Initially a 2-mill plant, it was almost immediately bought by Phelps, James & Co a Liverpool firm of buying/forwarding agents set up by Phelps Dodge, an American import/export agency, to buy British tinplate to satisfy the insatiable American demand for tinplate. Liverpool-based to handle the shipping, it drew almost all its requirements from South Wales, thus their south Wales representative, C. H. Brooke (father of that notable chronicler of the Industry. E H Brooke), was a very influential man indeed. Phelps James expanded Llangennech to 6-mills, turning out a product that established a quality bench-mark for all their tinplate purchases, which at the time amounted to the better part of half a million boxes per year or about 40% of total Welsh exports and perhaps 20% of the entire industry's production. Interestingly, in the 1930s the Metal Box Company, then the biggest single user of Welsh tinplate, bought the Eaglesbush works with the intention of raising and maintaining the standard of tinplate. The implication implicit in this was not appreciated by the rest of the industry.

In 1868 the Worcester was opened in Morriston by John Jones, William Williams and Daniel Edwards, all influential Morriston men. Edwards left after only two years to found his great Dyffryn works. The 10-mill Worcester amalgamated with the Upper Forrest works in 1898 to form a unit having 16 tinplate mills and 5 sheet mills.

In 1869 the Monmouth works opened but its situation, geared to an iron-forge and river transport brought an 1880s closure.

By 1870, with the demand for tinplate increasing almost exponentially, almost as many works would be opened in the next 20 years as had been opened in the previous 150 years. Moreover up to now, of the some 80 works in Britain, 30 had been outside south Wales and western Gloucestershire, being scattered around Scotland, north Wales and various English counties (mostly in the Midlands). Of the almost 70 works opened after 1873, only 3 would be outside South Wales, and none of those were started later than 1880.

With this intense expansion there were new location imperatives. In addition to the coal, dock and railway requirement, works needed to be near enough to existing tin works so that experienced labour might be poached and also near tinplate-orientated engineering establishments such as the various Llanelli ones, Millbrook at Swansea, Taylor at Briton Ferry and Neath Abbey Engineering. Thus overwhelmingly new openings would be located in west Glamorganshire and east Carmarthenshire.

Besides these locational changes Tinplate was on the cusp of a technical change that was as great a step forward as rolling had been in the 18th century and continuous strip operations would be in the 20th century – the replacement of iron with steel.

5

The Age of Steel

All manufacturing methods gradually evolve, in the case of traditional tinplate mill working, evolution was very gradual indeed. Steam power dates from the 17th century and electricity from the 19th, yet water wheels were turning tinplate mills post-WW2. Pack mills lasted for three decades after continuous-strip working was introduced. Cans were still being made by hand in parts of Europe in the 1950s, almost 100 years after the high speed mechanical can making machine had been invented. 'Charcoal Quality' defined the best tinplate, with 'Coke Quality' as a lesser standard long after those terms had ceased to have any metallurgical significance.

However, the switch from iron to steel was made in a timeframe that was by tinplate standards almost overnight.

Steel had been known from ancient times, but up to the mid-19th century, the laborious black art of converting iron to steel by the age-old crucible method could only be done in tiny batches and its cost confined it to special applications where performance was paramount, rather as applies to materials such as Titanium or Carbon Fibre today. Thus, as is still the case, the main use for such a material was military (Swords, armour and so on).

This was all changed when Bessemer and Siemens, developed ways of producing steel in bulk. Steel was more consistent than iron, its characteristics could be varied according to needs and the elimination of the labour-intensive puddling process needed to produce ductile iron, made steel potentially cheaper.

Bessemer had first produced steel in 1856 in Sheffield and as soon as the ink was dry on the patent, Dafen tinworks at Llanelli bought a licence, with the intention of setting up their own Bessemer plant, in the meantime going ahead with bars bought from Bessemer. For tinplate making these bars were a disaster and they hastily sold their licence. Nevertheless Ebbw Vale went ahead erecting plant under Sir Henry Bessemer's personal supervision in 1862. Three years later Dowlais followed suit and encouraged by the products of both works proving excellent for rails and girders, Aberdulais tinplate works tried using some Dowlais bars. As at Dafen, the steel proved of variable quality (some being so hard that it broke rolls) and yielded sheet that was of uneven temper. Since Bessemer steel was later successfully used and the process is the basis of all modern steel making, this not so much due to any shortcomings inherent in Bessemer steel as to inexperience and a failure to understand the benefits of alloy additives.

In the meantime at Swansea Dr C. W. Siemens, following extensive experimentation produced steel in 1861 in an Open-hearth process where pre-heated air was passed over molten iron as opposed to the more complex Bessemer converter method of spectacularly blowing air through the melt. Open-hearth was less costly to install and simpler to control. Siemens began commercial production in his own works at Landore in 1871 and a year later Alfred Sterry and Roger Beck built a works at Gowerton to operate Siemen's process, naming the works Elba since the island of Elba was then a new source of ore. Situated alongside a main line railway, adjacent to water and joined to a colliery by a dedicated railway line, it was very much 'State of the art'. A new steelworks at Panteg also offered tinbars.

Understandably the problems with Bessemer steel would deter an industry from trying any sort of steel, let alone an industry as 'change proof' as the tinplate industry then was, in any case many works were financially or geographically linked to iron producers. Thus Siemens had a thin time at Landore and at Gowerton the Elba works actually failed.

Nevertheless, despite an ongoing debate about steel, as has been said, the 1870s saw tinplate developments grow apace. In 1840 there were approximately 30 works making tinplate, by the start of the 1870s, there were around 60, by the end of the 1870's there were almost 90. A threefold increase in works numbers in four decades, but due to increased average size and improved methods, output had increased tenfold. By 1890 there would be something like 110 tinplate works.

The Franco-Prussian war brought commercial uncertainties that resulted in there being no new works in

Wales during 1870 and 1871, but come 1872 there were a then unprecedented four, all in the west. Octavius Williams manager of Hendy works for Webb, Shakespeare who previously had built the Morfa works at Llanelli, set up the 1-mill Glamorgan works at Pontardulais, eventually amalgamating it with the Hendy works as Webb, Shakespeare & Williams. Later as part of the Bynea group the Glamorgan had 4 mills mainly producing black plate. The Amman works at Brynamman was an iron works and forge that had been established in 1845 almost as soon as there had been railway connection to Llanelli. In 1872 Mr G. B. Strick took it over and put in first 3 then 4, tinplate mills. Like other works, located with iron rather than steel supplies in mind, it succumbed in 1897 and Strick's son took over the nearby Gyrnos works. Also in 1872 there was an unusual opening – the Gower works at Penclawdd. This 3-mill works mopped up the labour from the old copper works, whose site it occupied, but apart from having virtually direct connection to the Penclawdd Colliery, the situation had little to commend it. It managed to survive the problems of the 1880s, including the failure of the David Morris partnership but it could not survive long in the post-Mckinley era, closing in 1895.

More significant was the Morriston works. It was common for tin and other metallurgical works to 'Back integrate' with collieries to safeguard fuel supplies, but this was a 'Forward integration' by the Glasbrooks to provide a captive market for their coal. United with the Midland works it became a 13-mill company, that would survive until 1952, having been 're-forward integrated' in

1934 by the Briton Ferry Steel Co, as an outlet for their steel at a time when the tinworks were increasingly using low priced imported tinbars.

1873 saw two more works come on stream, the Mansel and the Morlais. The former at Port Talbot grew out of the purchase in 1864 of the old Margam tinplate works by Robert Byass and the erection of a new adjoining plant. By 1895 all work had been transferred to the newer premises making an 11-mill unit. that was a mainstay of the area's tinplate production until 1954. The Morlais at Llangennech was smaller, a 4-mill establishment that lasted until closed under the tinplate redundancy scheme at the end of WW2.

1874 saw the ancient ex-Parsons and ex Neath Abbey Iron Company, Clydach forge, lately owned by J. J. Strick; branch out into tinplating under John Player. This 4-mill works became part of a notable foundry and general engineering complex, that although it ceased to make tinplate during WW2, it did continue in business until the late 20th century. The Cambria at Pontardulais was opened by some local men as the Cambria Co-operative & Industrial Iron & Tinplate Manufacturing Company. Quite a mouthful for a 2-mill (Later 3-mill) works and again the same year the fine 15-mill Dyffryn integrated works at Morriston was opened by W. H. Edwards, who also started the 4-mill Ely works at Llantrisant. This latter was one of the few examples of tinplate manufacture in mid-Glamorgan and underlines the difficulty in finding rail-served sites close to collieries. The valleys were becoming choked, some having canals and roads as well as railways, (virtually stacked four high at Walnut Tree in the Taff valley), as well as collieries and sundry other industries.

More radically sited was the south Wales owned, 3-mill Alyn works at Mold. Although workers were available from the recently closed cotton mill whose site it occupied and from the decline of lead mining. Despite an absence of tinplate tradition and of engineering and other support, this 'out-on-a-limb' enterprise, after some initial vicissitudes proved surprisingly durable, ending up in the Richard Thomas Group.

More significant was the Tynewydd works opened the same year. It was an unremarkable 3-mill outfit in the now increasingly unfashionable Monmouthshire valleys, but after being taken over and re-equipped by the Redbrook Company, it became in 1904 the first tinplate works in the world to be fully electrically driven. In addition a tin box factory, the Pontnewydd Tin Stamping became a very early example of forward integration by a tinplate concern. When directed onto munitions work in WW1 it developed a lacquering for shell making that was widely applied at other ordnance factories. Surviving total destruction by fire in 1918 it did not close until WW2.

1875 saw the opening at Pontardulais of the Clayton works, an establishment that acquired a cachet well beyond its 7-mill size and that same year the (eventually 4-mill) Aberavon was opened. It had an interesting history, its ancestry traceable to 1839 when the Porthcawl, Iron & Coal company started, shortly re-inventing itself as the Patent Galvanised Iron Co. that ceased trading in 1850. Again in 1875, the previously mentioned Burry at

Llanelli opened and the following year, the 4-mill Gyrnos works at Lower Cwmtwrch, that would later be run by Percy Player of Clydach.

With the old water power-abundant valleys of Monmouthshire, ceasing to be the location of choice for new tinplate works, the 1877 opening of the (eventually) 6-mill Avondale at Pontnewydd was one of the last in the Newport hinterland. Although headed by John Paton it was never part of the Partridge, Jones and John Paton group. The other opening that year was the 4-mill Resolven, in the rather more spacious Vale of Neath. It was later absorbed by the Briton Ferry Steel Company as part of a policy of forward integration to create 'captive' customers.

In 1878 the 6-mill Cilfrew works was opened just across the valley from Resolven by the Gething brothers who probably had been connected with iron working. Reduced to 2 mills it later became part of the Richard Thomas group. This was the only tinplate works opened in 1878, reflecting a plateau in the advance of tin, but there was coming an event that would turn the industry on its head, revitalise it and create an unseemly stampede of openings and the great 1880s tinplate boom.

By this time steel was gradually displacing iron as a substrate, mainly due to that most powerful of arguments – lower prices, although in some ways lower steel prices were counterproductive, causing it to be seen by some as a cheap substitute for iron. Partly to overcome this prejudice, the old descriptions remained in use. 'Coke' still denoted a standard quality with 'Charcoal', 'Best

Charcoal' and even 'Best Best Charcoal' denoting the better qualities. Similarly right into the strip mill era, even when tinplate was being sold in coils, the thickness of tinplate was expressed as 'Substance' a term derived from the weight of a Basis Box of 512 square feet.

Anyway the event that would totally blow away the prejudice against steel occurred at the Paris Exhibition of 1878, where Bliss & Williams, the American press makers, demonstrated a new sardine-can making machine. Since this machine made severe demands on the tinplate, the very best wrought iron based tinplate was used rather than trusting the new-fangled steel-based article for this important occasion. The demonstration was a humiliating disaster the cans splitting as they were formed. That is until samples were produced by Phelps, James & Company of Llangennech Work's 'Best Charcoal' *St George* Brand, made from the first batch of steel tinbars produced at the Elba steelworks recently reopened by Wright, Butler and Company. Every can made from this steel was perfect.

With the can makers demanding steel, the whole character of the Tinplate Industry changed. The blast and puddling furnaces cooled into industrial monuments, cenotaphs to an age that was suddenly bygone. Few tinplate makers would have the room, and even fewer the money to erect steelworks, so they would be left to scramble on the open market for supplies of steel bar. Interestingly at Llanelli in 1879, the Marshfield works that was not doing too well was bought into by a curious syndicate of Ernest Trubshaw, WH Forrester, a Swansea metal merchant presumably seeking security of supply, John Powell of the Glanmor Foundry (who was also a director of Old Castle), J. J. Jenkins (Lord Glantawe), Byng Morris (of Morriston fame), plus J. T. Smith (Brother-in-law of Trubshaw) of the Barrow Iron and steel Company; they traded as the Western Tin Plate Works. Whether they had ideas of going into steel making at the time is not known but in the event they did not but nevertheless they prospered mightily adding by the end of the 1880's an additional 5 mills. In 1898 they, in partnership with the Old Castle works and the Briton Ferry Steel Company, formed the Llanelly Steel Company.

This was a clear manifestation of the fact that there was no place for the small independent works anachronistically surviving on a site based on water-powered forge needs, thus the mighty Melingriffith with its 6 sheet mills and 12 tinplate mills, its numerous waterwheels backed up by steam engines, its owners Booker having just formed a £550,000 Company with Gilbertson of Pontardawe collapsed under a mountain of debt in 1879. It was picked up by Richard Thomas for a mere £22,500. At least he did restart it, other iron-based works, mostly in Monmouthshire closed for good. Parkend and Tydu both closed in 1881, Gilwern in 1884, Pontnewydd a year later and Monmouth a year after that and Rhiwderin in 1886.

Partridge, Jones and John Paton maintained a Gwent presence partly by building their own steelworks and similarly Richard Thomas's Lydney steelworks (and the small but adjacent Lydney docks) kept the Lydney tinplate works in business.

Generally however all this gave a further impetus to the westward march of tinplate, now not just seeking space, coal, rails and docks, but also sources of steel, which would be predominately at the western end of the coalfield.

Open-hearth furnaces abounded, some as 'Add-ons' by the iron makers, others as 'backward-integration' by combinations of tinplate men, seeking control of price and quality and continuity of supply. Within 2 years of the Paris demonstration four new steelworks opened dedicated to the manufacture of tinbars the basic diet of the tinplate works. The Millbrook foundry at Landore fired up an open-hearth furnace in 1880, and Mr (later Sir) Richard Martin started another at Birchgrove. These did not last long but the other two that started up that same year were more firmly founded. The aforementioned Partridge, Jones and John Paton's steelworks alongside their Pontymister tinworks supplied the group up until 1952 and the South Wales works at Llanelli that turned out tinbars until 1958.

The tinbar market became very volatile. With the expansion in demand for steel, a shortage would develop so a new steelworks would be opened, typically with a rolling mill that could supply up to 50 tin mills, thus creating a surplus that depressed prices until demand caught up. Then someone would open yet another steelworks and the cycle would be repeated. Cwmbwrla tinplate works had their own steel plant by 1882, but it proved uneconomic so from 1898 they bought in their requirements. The next year the tinworks at Melyn at Neath and in 1884 the Morfa at Llanelli, each had steel plants, but like the Trimsaran Steelworks of 1885, all had succumbed to competition from the big steelworks by the end of the century.

The other 1885 steelworks opening, the Cwmfelin was more durable and like the Pontymister plant it was a large works, selling surplus production to other tinplate works and later functioned as an internal supplier for the Richard Thomas combine and as such lasted until 1957. The Castle works at Rogerstone was smaller but despite being in what was now an unfashionable site for steelworking, survived until 1921.

Although Cwmbwrla had shown that a steelworks small enough to be dedicated to supplying one tinplate works was a non-starter the Copper Miners Company at Cwmavon opened their Express steel works in 1889, unsurprisingly it closed after a mere four years. In 1890 there were three new steelworks catering for the tinplate trade Grovesend, Briton Ferry and Gilbertson's at Pontardawe, the latter being followed the next year by integrations at Morriston by Dyffryn in 1893 and Upper Forest and Worcester in 1896.

By this time the opening in 1893 of the Albion steelworks had added to the Briton Ferry area's steel capacity and four years later Bryngwyn works brought more steel making capacity to the expanding Pontardulais/Gorseinon tinbar demands. The steel output of Llanelli's South Wales works was massively augmented in 1898 by the Llanelly Steelworks and in 1912 by the very last tinplate orientated steelworks, Bynea in which the Tregonings had a substantial interest.

6

The Great Crescendo

The eight new tinplate works in 1879 meant that a new opening occurred every six weeks, half of them in the Swansea valley, suggesting a quite extraordinary challenge to man them. Phoenix (Gilwen) at Lower Cwmtwrch and Glanyrafon (Park) at Clydach both had 3 mills, but Bryn at Ynysmedw peaked at 5 mills (including 3 for black plate and galvanised sheet). The Glanrhyd with which the Gilbertsons augmented their Pontardawe capacity had 6 mills.

These all did well but the other four were less successful. Dowlais steelworks' brief attempt at diversification into tinplate proved unfortunate as did the 4-mill Hawkwell works that the Kidwelli proprietors set up just into Gloucestershire at Cinderford which was almost immediately dismantled, this latter indicating that Monmouthshire and the Forest of Dean was no longer a viable location. The 3 (or 4?) mill Caldicot works right alongside the Great Western main line was more successful, but with the Severn Tunnel contractors paying big money at the time, labour must have been a problem until the tunnel was finished ten years later. This oddly sited works ceased to make tinplate at the end of the century, reinventing itself as a stamping and enamelling works in conjunction with the Avondale tinplate works. This was one of the few instances of a tinplate works 'forward integrating into 'downstream' manufacture. The big, bold, 7-mill Blaina works, one of the P. S. Phillips clutch, although again ironworks based in Monmouthshire was coalfield located so did better, eventually having 11 mills until felled by the McKinley Tariff.

This expansion was aided by the comparative cheapness of entry into tinplate. Being a modular industry built around the (Hot) mill, setting up might cost less than £3000. Additional modules could be added, but the benefits of scale was not necessarily great, so 2-mill tiddlers could with skilful management, compete with larger works. This made tinplate an attractive investment for comparatively modest professional men and tradesmen but could result in sitings that were cheap and local with little regard for practicality. Ownership could be very 'hands on', but there tended to be little interest in expansion, development or innovation with a regrettable reluctance to establish sinking funds to meet depreciation. More significantly, working capital needs were minimal. Tinplate was sold on a spot cash basis and although wages (say around 80 men per mill) had to be paid, tin was bought on credit that might extend to as much as nine months, whilst the rolling mills would often grant a year's credit on tinbars. Thus regardless of profitability there was likely to be a temptation to share out surplus cash, a recipe for disaster if trade took a downturn.

However with prospects being extrapolated to infinity, downturns were unthinkable and in 1880 there were eight more new works. Abbey Tintern works was a 2-mill reuse of a century-old forge site, but like Hawkwell it was too 'out on a limb' so scarcely outlasted it. Also on a disused forge site and outside the now mainstream tinplate area was the Lion works at Nantyglo started by west Glamorgan men including one of the Gethings. It lasted a year and restarted as the Nantyglo works under P. S. Phillips, who owned Abertillery, Pontymister and Waterloo works as well as a part interest in Blaina, it prospered to become a respectable 8-mill outfit. When in 1896 at the height of the 'McKinley blight', Phillips ceased trading, the works was taken by the Swansea Tinplate Co, who also owned the Cwmfelin, Aber and Cynon works. Although obtained at a knockdown price Swansea could not make it pay and closed it in 1902.

The other 1880 start-ups were all in the west, conventionally sited for rails and coal, and although the 2-mill Birchgrove would close in 1895, the rest, the 6-mill Old Lodge at Llanelli and the 8-mill Aber at Llansamlet would prove more durable, although the former suffered some vicissitudes twice failing, the second time in 1882 when the David Morris syndicate went under.

The remaining 1880 works was syncophantly named, as was the adjacent public house, after the landowner, Lord Dynevor. It was originally sponsored by Mr Foden of Sandbach in Cheshire and sited near a settlement named Cross Inn after the crossroads pub that was its principal feature. His firm was supplier of steam mill engines, this connection presumably drawing his attention to the fact that tinplate was a 'Good thing to get into'. His firm was later famed as a maker of heavy lorries, a reputation later to be overtaken by its brass band. Siting alongside Pantyffynon colliery ensured the fuel supply and the transport needs would be catered for by the adjacent London & North Western Railway that was bringing prosperity to the village that would shortly be distinguished from the numerous other 'Cross Inns' by being renamed Ammanford. The location was near enough to the then declining forges of the upper Loughor River to ensure a supply of labour used to hot-metal work.

Despite these good auguries Mr Foden backed off and the project was taken over by a group of local men who floated the Dynevor Tin Plate & Iron Company. They were Evan Williams a farmer from nearby Betws, David Hushe a local draper, James Davies a draper from Llandilo and Rees Thomas, a timber merchant, represented the increasing participation of local, modest men with a 'Shilling or two put by'. Increasingly the metaphorical butcher or baker were getting into tinplate, seemingly not just as a source of income but to generate trade for their own businesses. Right up to the end of the 19th century in certain works although no formal 'Truck' was in operation, if one of the owners was a retailer, it was advisable to make ones' purchases with him.

To provide expertise, they took on board David Thomas an iron founder, Enoch Stanford a tinplate manager both from Pontardulais and Trevor Davies also described as a manager' from Llangennech (Tinplate works?)

This 3-mill Dynevor that brought tinplate manufacture to a new area of the coalfield, was later taken over by the influential Grovesend Steel and Tinplate Company headed by Henry Folland. Folland, was one of the many men such as Gibbin and William Williams who started as ordinary employees, but whose shrewdness and luck took them into top management and ownership, or as in the case of Richard Thomas to found a great combine, or J. J. Jenkins who achieved ennoblement.

Old Lodge at Llanelli has already been mentioned, but another important opening was the 8-mill Teilo works that gave further impetus to the growth of Pontardulais. Although there had been several forges and other water-powered industry along the river Dulais, 'The Bont' itself had been described as a bridge with a pub at each end, in fact the population of the (extensive) parish of Llandeilo Talybont was less than 600. The opening of the Llanelly Railway & Dock Company's line in 1839 meant that it's prosperity was assured. Confirmation of this bright industrial future came in 1866 when the railway to Swansea via Gorseinon and Gowerton was built, making Pontardulais an important junction. Sadly this line has closed but the original line, the first 'Full Sized' railway in Wales is still in business and still using the Pontardulais tunnel, also the first in Wales. Sadly the once flourishing four-platform station, handling cattle, coal, agricultural products and all the necessities of a booming town as well as a torrent of tinplate, is reduced to a single-platform, unmanned 'Bus Stop'. Only a year after this latter line opened, the Graig Merthyr colliery raised its first drams of coal. By the end of the 19th century the powerful triumvirate of the Hendy, the Clayton and now the Teilo works pushed the population to near 6000.

When in 1910 they were joined by the 4-mill Dulais and the 6-mill Glynhir, the town had almost 40 mills and a population that would shortly show a twenty-fold increase on its pre-industrial figure. Although there was some immigration from Bristol and elsewhere, mainly to the chemical works, the tinplate industry needed experienced workers so the bulk of the incomers that created this population explosion came from within Wales. Thus the town remained a bastion not only of the language, but also of every aspect of Welsh culture.

Each working day they would produce almost 400 tons or enough tinplate in a week to put a layer over the entire town. In 6 months their output would encircle the earth. Not perhaps exciting figures in modern strip-mill terms, but when one realises that each day approaching a million sheets had each been handled and re-handled a dozen times, these figures seem less mundane.

There were four new works in 1881; the 5-mill Raven and its associated 4-mill Amman were erected not far from the Dynevor and also became part of the Grovesend combine. The big (9 Tinplate mills and 10 sheet mills) Gorseinon works proved slightly financially fraught but was rescued by the Grovesend Company. Similarly the Ffrwdwyllt at Port Talbot with 3 and later 5 mills would owe its survival to being taken over by the Briton Ferry Steel Company.

There were no openings until the ephemeral Neath Abbey works of 1885 and in 1886, the Fairwood and the Grovesend that like the Gorseinon works took advantage of the Pontardulais – Swansea railway. Fairwood a 4-mill works was financially tied in with the Clayton and the Teilo at Pontardulais, but was actually sited at Gowerton, presumably to tap a new pool of labour. Grovesend became an integrated Steel/tinplate works with 10 tinplate mills and the hub of the Grovesend combine. In addition, on the wave of optimism, the Tregonings virtually totally re-equipped the Morfa works at Llanelli.

In 1888 the Villiers was opened at Briton Ferry by the Briton Ferry Steel Company and the same year, despite it having been recognised that the Eastern Valleys were no longer appropriate places to make tinplate the ephemeral Trevor works opened at Pontypool; it did not last long and possibly never produced. The next year the 8-mill, Baglan Bay opened and the 3-mill Aberlash at Tirydail augmented the increasingly industrially fashionable Glanaman and Ammanford area. It is said that its sponsor, Colonel Jones fancied the neighbouring Dyffryn Mansion, but it was not on the market, so Jones (allegedly) went over to 3-shift working to (successfully) encourage the owner to sell!

The Ynyscedwyn at Ystradgynlais was a small (3-mill) tinplate works with an interesting pedigree. The 18th century Ynyscedwyn 6-furnace iron works was where David Thomas manager under George Crane had in 1836, first smelted iron with anthracite coal. Arising out of this, work was started in the USA, David Thomas being (rightly) regarded as the founder of the Pennsylvania Iron and Steel industry. By the 1880s the demand for iron was wilting under the advance of steel and although an attempt was made to set up an Open-Hearth steel plant, more luck was eventually had with a 3-mill tinplate works built on the site in 1889. The Ynyscedwyn Company failed, but in 1905 the Ynscedwyn Tin Plate Company re-activated the tinplate department, surviving until 1939 when it was briefly reconstituted as the Anglo Welsh Tinplate Co.

In 1890 the pace of new openings recovered; besides the already mentioned Ashburnham at Burry Port, there were five others. The Eagle, (later Eaglesbush) at Neath, with ultimately 7 mills, plus 2 sheet mills (also used for tinplate) was the largest and for a time was owned by Baldwins the great Midlands Ironmaster family; a scion of which became Prime Minister. The 4-mill Wern was built at Briton Ferry by Mr Stanford using plant bought from the then recently closed Rhiwderin works. This works had a somewhat bumpy ride through the 1890s passing through various hands including the Albion Steel Company, becoming also part of Baldwins in 1923. The 3-mill (later 4-mill) Cardonnel at Skewen in which colliery proprietor John H. Strick had an interest, took the family name of the landowner Lord Dynevor. Ideally situated close to the railway and Skewen Main colliery it was a mainstay employer for Skewen, later becoming part of the Richard Thomas combine.

The Glynbeudy was a 4-mill works established at Brynaman by the Gilbertsons of Pontardawe, presumably in anticipation of them being able to deliver steel to it via the then proposed railway link from the increasingly brisk Aman valley area to Pontardawe. The works was sold to a Neath syndicate in 1917, by which time it was clear that the part-built line would never be completed. The Gilbertsons bought Glynbeudy back ten years later by which time deliveries by motor-lorry were practicable.

Pentyrch works at Taffs Well near Cardiff, the old iron tinbar supplier to Ynyspenllwch and Melingriffith tinplate works, was still surviving in the iron business in quite a big way but by the mid late 1870s with their local sources of ore succumbing to foreign competition, the failure of the West of England and District bank brought about their demise in 1879. the Melingriffith works was taken by James Spence but the Pentyrch site failed to find a buyer, the landlord seized the property and let it to Waterhouse Bros a Bradford firm of iron domestic hollowware makers. They apparently set up a tinplate making works here in 1890 but what they produced is unclear, in any case by 1915 they had surrendered the lease. The site was taken on in 1930 by The Pentyrch Steel & Tinplate Company but they went out of business the next year, probably without ever producing anything. Melingriffith took over but it is not known if they did any tinning. What is clear is that this would be the last tinplate pack mill to be erected east of Port Talbot. This was partly due to the lack of sites in the tight-packed valleys of east south Wales, but more to the fact that the Siemens steel works were overwhelmingly being concentrated in the west, making the delivered price of tinbars in the east Glamorgan/Monmouthshire region slightly dearer, but in those days of wafer-thin profit margins the difference between profit and loss.

By 1890 the Welsh tinplate industry could look back on two decades that had seen tinplate production quadruple, the half-million tons of annual output mark having passed unnoticed. In a dozen years the tonnage passing through Swansea docks had increased by well over 3000%. The count of works neared 100 and the number of mills, including plate mills, nudged 500. The tinplate juggernaut seemed unstoppable, but there was 'Writing on the Wall' and as is invariably the case when such is script is manifest, there is collective myopia.

7

Tinplate - The Gotterdamrung

Casserite the main ore of tin is not found in the USA. This may have contributed to the American tinplate industry being slow to develop, leading to its being overwhelmed by the explosive growth of tinplate use from the mid 19th century. Just as had been the case in Britain 300 years earlier, an infant industry could not compete with a large and mature foreign source.

By the late 19th century the United States was a highly industrialised country and the world's greatest user of tinplate in every form. There was a strong Welsh connection, partly through Welshmen being poached for their skills but also due to the success of Mormon proselytization in Wales. An example being B. J. Davies Job, who with his sons established the Davis Dairy Machine Company and other firms in Chicago, that in the wake of the Civil War established a near monopoly of every sort of dairy requirement right across the USA. Almost every machine and vessel being made of tinplate – Welsh tinplate, much from their hometown of Carmarthen.

Whilst the fiercely patriotic Davies' might be proud to support Welsh industry, others were not, in any case for

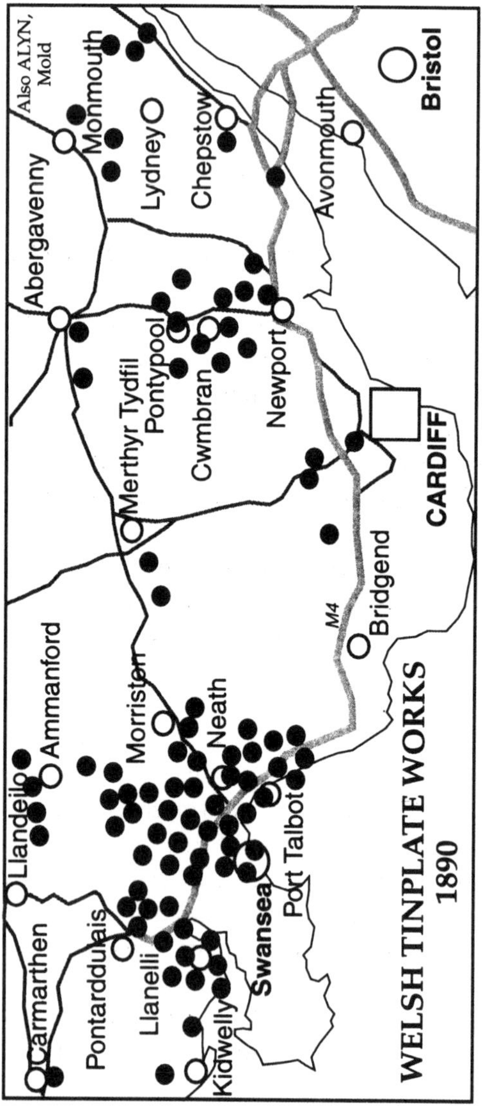

WELSH TINPLATE WORKS
1890

such a nation to be dependent on imported supplies did not make political or economic sense. Traditionally protectionist, the American instinct was to deal with every economic problem by building a tariff barrier around it.

In the late 1880s Congressman William McKinley from Ohio, a Republican backed by big business interests proposed a 50% increase on import duties on a range of manufactured goods including tinplate. Whilst the passing of this through Congress was welcomed by the tinplate industry, the general public was not best pleased with the price hikes that this brought about and McKinley ignominiously lost his seat at the next election, (although he bounced back later to become President).

With America taking almost two-thirds of Welsh output, when the Act came into effect in 1891 the effect was catastrophic, its impact exaggerated by American merchants having bought in ahead of the Act's implementation. This coupled with an easing in the home market, plus the plethora of new works that had come on stream in the recent past, turned a recession into a depression, a setback into devastation.

The previous 20 years had seen Welsh production quadruple to 600,000 tons, within three years it had all but halved.

Works slashed their prices in a vain endeavour to remain competitive in the American market, even so most went onto short time working or left some of their mills idle. Either of these courses increased their basic per-box costs, further adding to their problems. Business failures abounded, not only in the tinplate firms themselves but also creditor suppliers. By the end of the decade half the works had closed completely, some never to re-open, with in some cases, their machinery sold to America where demand was running ahead of supply. In 1892 the USA produced 18,000 tons of tinplate, in 1906 577,000 tons and by 1916 output exceeded a million tons. (British tons not American Short Tons!) By contrast Welsh exports to the USA dropped from well over 300,000 tons in 1890, to less than 20,000 tons by 1900, dropping to a nominal 1000 tons by 1916. Phelps James & Co who had handled a million and a half boxes in 1890, had by 1900 virtually withdrawn from the tinplate business.

Morewood & Company who still had extensive Midlands interests in forging and other manufacture, finding their Llanelli and Swansea works badly hit, reacted boldly by opening large works at Elizabeth Port, New Jersey and in Gas City Indian.

Those works that closed permanently in the post-McKinley era were Trevor (1892), Avonvale, Neath Abbey, Birchgrove, Gower and Hawkwell (1895), Caldicott (1896), Ynyspenllwch and Amman (1897), Carmarthen (1899), Blaina and Maesteg (1900), Abbey Tintern and Landore (1901), Lion (1902), Aberlash (1908). Caldicott and Ynyspenllwch found new careers as canister makers. Works as ill sited as Carmarthen, Lion, Maesteg and Ynsypenllwch were past hope, but many reopened, usually under new owners, having bought the assets at knockdown prices. As exampled by the 'Management buyout' of the South Wales works at Llanelli and the Cwmbrwla works at Swansea by F. W. & H. C. Bond who had been partners in the company. The Cambria at

Pontardulais having long abandoned its co-operative status, was bought by the Bryngwyn Steel Company, presumably to ensure that at least one works remained in business to buy their tinbars. Hendy works had been taken over in 1888 by J. Cound and Basil Jayne lately of the ephemeral Brynmawr tinplate works, but in 1892 it fell victim to the McKinley tariff but was restarted by the splendidly named Webb, Shakespeare & Co. It later became part of the Grovesend Steel Company. Llangennech works having suffered some setbacks since Phelps, James sold it in 1881 failed in 1899 but was restarted in 1901.

Such new owners have been criticised for profiting from other's misfortunes, but it was only their buying in at prices that enabled working to be profitable that ensured continued employment. Even though tin prices were at an all-time low and the cost of tinbars was well down, having to sell tinplate at around 60% of 1890s prices was not a recipe for riches.

These factors helped to make the most marginal economies of scale the difference between profit and loss, ushering in the era of the big combines, with amalgamations and takeovers continuing into the 1930s, mostly nucleated around a steelworks.

To revert to the 'Nineties', the hedonistic extravagance for which the decade is proverbial was not in evidence in the tinplate districts. In places such as Pontardulais, and the Amman valley with their recently established works, men found themselves laid off as fast as they had so recently been taken on. The spanking new tinplate-dedicated Prince of Wales dock at Swansea found its quays seriously depleted. By the end of the decade tinplate was fetching little more than half its 1890 prices, and about than a third of the 1870s average.

The Raven works at Glanaman survived by going into the Grovesend group and converting to galvanising work. The Aberavon quickly diversified into galvanising, although this did not last long and they sold out this side of the business to the Phoenix Galvanising and Corrugating Co, ensuring their own survival by going in for stamping, re-registering as the Aberavon Tinplate and Stamping Co in 1899.

In fact the growth of 'Corrugated Iron' as a building material and the replacement of cast iron by galvanised metal for such things as rainwater goods, substantially mitigated the loss of tinplate sales. The growth of the rightly reviled 'Shanty towns' of sub-Saharan Africa would prove a useful market for galvanised sheet. The tale is told of a representative visiting South Africa and finding that much corrugated sheet was beaten flat before use. He telegraphed his works and set about stealing a march on his competitors by marketing 'Ready flattened' galvanised sheet. The exercise was a total failure – he had not realised that the corrugated sheet was being flattened to increase its width! At the same time some new markets for tinplate were developed such as the 'Crown' cap as a replacement for the 'glass-ball' bottle stopper.

However in the meantime life went on. In a spirit of 'Crisis, what crisis?' Gwalia opened its 4 mills at Briton Ferry in 1892 and soldiered on under the Briton Ferry flag. Apart from this, while the industry rode out the storm, no new tinplate works would open.

Some small steelworks such as Millbrook, Morfa and Trimsaran, robbed of their main customer base, closed permanently after a mere decade or so of operation. Cwmbwrla found it more economic to buy in tinbars from nearby Cwmfelin, similarly Copper Miners at Cwmafon closed their Express steelworks.

Despite orders from America, the specialist tinplate machinery makers such as Glanmor Foundry at Llanelli. Millbrook at Swansea and Taylor Bros at Briton Ferry, found their order books thin, with second-hand equipment being available for such requirements as there were.

In 1897 fresh demand for black plate was created when the Welsh Tinplate and Metal Stamping Co, opened up on the disused site of the old Cambrian Copper works at Llanelli, to produce a range of enamelled ware that would make the 'Goat' brand world famous. As has been mentioned, the next year two of the Llanelli tinplate works, the Old Castle and the Western, teamed up with Briton Ferry Steel seeking to increase their competitiveness by building the fine Llanelly Steel Works.

The new century brought hope but little else. With the shakeout in the industry eliminating the desperation discounts, prices on the home market at least recovered but the cost of tin and tinbars had gone through the roof. The employment situation was not eased by the arrival of men fleeing the declining north Wales slate quarries. (Their loss of markets having been exacerbated by the increasing use of south Wales galvanised sheets!)

Paradoxically, the USA having virtually wrecked the Welsh tinplate industry, were at least partly responsible for its resurgence. The motorcar might have been a European invention but it was America that made it affordable, and quite apart from the need for steel sheet in every form for the vehicles themselves, the containers for motor transport's fuel, lubricants and unction's of every kind created a whole new market for tinplate.

Besides this, indigenous canning of soft fruits, fish and soups helped tinplate to get back on its feet. It is remarkable that only thirteen years after McKinley, output matched the 12 million box 1890 level and in less than two decades other markets had fully replaced the loss of American orders. Unfortunately at a cost, since America was now a competitor in exports forcing prices down so that although tonnages had recovered to pre-McKinley levels revenues definitely had not.

In an interesting grouping that was not so much a group as a common ownership arrangement, the Llanelly Steel Works was reconstituted with a number of tinplate works as shareholders. These, Clayton, Dafen, Eaglesbush, Ferry, Gyrnos, Melyn, Morlais, Old Lodge, John Player, St David's and Teilo (the position of Western is unclear) each apparently taking up shares in proportion to their number of mills. Briton Ferry Steel retained an interest until 1934.

The establishment of the Neath Sheet Steel & Galvanising Company in 1896 had shown how works were increasingly looking to non-tin products. This was emphasised in 1908 when the Grovesend Company opened the 4-mill Wellfield works purely to produce zinc sheets and again three years later with the opening of the 5-mill Gorse Galvanising works. With a strengthening demand for black plate as well as galvanised products, the Whitford Steel Sheet & Galvanising Co. was set up at Briton Ferry.

As far as actual tinplate was concerned, many temporarily closed works had reopened but such was the pressure on profits that it was 1910 before the first totally new opening took place, the 'State of the Art', all electric, 14-mill King's Dock works built not by local interests but the already huge Baldwin's group, the sole example of a totally new build by a big firm. As if encouraged by this, the 6-mill Mardy at Gorseinon, the 4 mill Dulais and the 6-mill Glynhir at Pontardulais, were all opened the same year and in 1911 the 3-mill Pemberton at Llanelli. All were set up by local businessmen, reflecting the increasing prosperity of the area and save for the Mardy, which became part of the Grovesend combine, all remained independent until their eventual closure. In addition Richard Thomas opened the 8-mill R.T.Mills, adjoining their Bury and South Wales works to make a mighty 34 mill complex.

It is interesting to note how the McKinley disaster and the subsequent resurgence further concentrated the industry into Wales. In 1891 of the 98 British works and 525 mills 7 works and 19 mills (7% & 3.6% respectively) were outside Wales and south Gloucestershire, by 1905 of the 83 works and 453 mills 3 works and 11 mills (3.6% & 2.4%) would be outside Wales and South Gloucestershire.

However times remained fiercely competitive and the unswerving belief held by all tinplate workers, that one's own works made the best tinplate became even more dogmatic. These people, when challenged to give some technical explanation for a particular brand's superiority would invariably fall back on a terse– 'It Just Is! OK!' and turn the conversation to other things. Since sardine cans demanded the best deep-drawing grade, the greatest boast a tinplate worker could make was that his works' product was the tinplate of choice for 'Skippers' (Sardines) and it was said that managers would put it about that they would be working on 'Skippers' orders to keep the workers on their toes. Not all orders were welcomed on the shop floor, Tate & Lyle being a particularly unpopular name. (Golden Syrup tins were of heavier gauge than other food cans).

Each works offered a dozen or more of brands, as fancifully named as racehorses. Charcoal denoted the better qualities, with Coke describing lesser grades, amongst a superfluity superlatives, the term Best finished up almost as an indication of mediocrity. The main difference in quality was the thickness of tin coating but ductility for pressing came into it, classified as Ordinary, Deep Stamping and Deep Drawing. Besides this plethora of Prime grades, less than perfect products were offered as Menders, Wasters or Waste Waste, depending on the degree of defect. The commonest 'Substance' was 108lb (0.122" thick) with up to 256lb being offered (0.288"). Thinner 'Substances' such as 50lb (0.056") were classed as Taggers.

8

Tinplate in and between the Wars

Although from 1893 to 1908 there were no new tinplate works built, re-openings and expansions reflected the recovery in selling prices that the new century brought, although much of the increase was swallowed up by a sharp rise in tin. There was a slight setback in this recovery in 1906, but this soon gave way to renewed demand. Thus when the six new tinplate works of 1909-1911 came on stream they found plenty of custom, with even exports buoyant and Swansea docks alone loading in the order of 25,000 boxes per day. This turnaround was in some measure due to the effectiveness of the Tinplate Association, which since the 1890s had ensured that the industry projected a united front to the world, speaking with one voice to governments, customers and to the public.

In 1914 the trade was looking forward to a fourth consecutive 16-million box year. The shooting of a duke, arch or ordinary, in an obscure Balkan town the previous day can scarcely have taken precedence over the Swans, the All Whites and the weather as a topic of conversation in the cafes of Wind Street or the bar of the Metropole Hotel, Swansea, on a hot Monday in June. But of course the effect was cataclysmic.

Exports were hit and by 1917 when the U-Boat 'sink on sight' policy really took effect they were down by almost two thirds to levels not seen since the 1870s. Food shortages and manufacturing restrictions reduced domestic consumption, but rations for the armed forces maintained home demand. In the trenches a relief from the horrors was the opportunity to prise open a can of 'Corned Dog' with a bayonet. Soldiers guarding the Rock of Gibraltar would parody the reply to the traditional dusk ceremonial challenge 'Whose Keys?' with 'Maconochie's'. (A reference to a nutritious but not universally relished canned concoction of meat and vegetables, first supplied to troops during the Boer War. Indeed there were barrack-room myths in WW1 and even WW2 that over-ordered stock from the Boer War was still being issued!)

Government controls and a shortage of raw materials rather than shortage of orders reduced tinplate output by around 60%. The scarcest item was coal, every possible lump of south Wales steam coal was speeded north by the 'Jellicoe Special' trains to the Fleet at Scapa Floe. Richard Thomas and several independent works bought collieries to try to ensure supplies, but with men going to the forces, a tragically large proportion never to return, and despite a considerable increase in women workers, it was shortage of labour that became the biggest constraint to output, although save Ponthir all works apparently survived the war.

The men who did return came back not only to a much-changed industry, but also a much-changed society as perhaps illustrated by the Edwards Morriston dynasty.

Daniel Edwards had brought industry (and the great Tabernacl Chapel) to Morriston. His son W.H. had developed that industry but his son Sir John Bryn Edwards sold out in 1920 to live the country squire's life at Hendrefoilan House, the erstwhile home of that earlier great industrialist Lewis Dillwyn. As a further manifestation of the changes in society, Dillwyn's daughter Amy who famously and successfully took over her father's enterprises saw the daughter of Corfield her works manager marry Sir John to become not only chatelaine of her old family home but a 'Lady' to boot.

Towards the end of the war, in 1917 & 1918 respectively, the Richard Thomas group had acquired the Cwmfelin works, and Richard Nevil & Co, the Llanelli suppliers of steel rolls etc. Although Richard Thomas himself had died the Richard Thomas Company had clearly maintained the founder's prescience in anticipating a post-war boom for which such additional assets would be invaluable. Indeed tinplate prices began a climb that took them to three times pre-war levels. Similarly Henry Folland of the Grovesend Steel & Tinplate Co. had an eye to the future when he took over the Whitford Galvanising Co in 1916, and snapped up the Gorseinon and the Cambria (Pontardulais) tinplate works and the Bryngwyn steel and sheet works in 1919 before the extent of the boom was fully apparent. Folland further increased the strength of the group by buying into the Glasbrook Coal Company and the Llanelli Foundry and Engineering Company.

Not surprisingly the high prices of tinplate had not escaped the notice of the workers, nor had the high prices in the shops escaped the notice of their wives.

Wages had gone up, but only by 25% since 1874 an increase that in no way reflected the increase in the cost of living

	1874	1920
Rollermen	3/5 (17.1p)	4/3_ (21.2p)
Doubler	2/9 (13.7p)	3/5_ (17.2p)
Furnaceman	2/7 (12.9p)	3/2_ (16.2p)
1st Helper	2/5 (12.1p)	3/0_ (15.1p)
2nd Helper	1/8 (8.3p)	2/1 (10p)
Behinder	1/5 (7.1)	1/9½ (9.7p)
Shearers	1/1 (5.4p)	1/4½ (6.9p)
All per dozen boxes		
The openers' rates were Per 1000 sheets	7/0 (35p)	9/8½ (48.4p)

There was unrest, but there were none of the confrontations that soured other heavy industries. That this was the case was due to the Tinplate Conference. This body had been set up in the previous century to deal with all internal matters including labour-relations disputes that could not be settled at works level and also negotiated wages and conditions agreements with the unions. The manifest abilities and integrity of both the employer and the union members of Conference enabled tinplate to have better labour relations than any other comparable industry. Their one failure was their inability, by the narrowest of margins to obtain union agreement to a pioneering industry-wide pension scheme.

Actually the boom proved largely illusory, the sudden demand for tin and for tinbars, sent the prices of both through the roof. This coupled with a backlog of plant repairs and renewals meant that profits in tinplate manufacture remained elusive, although Baldwins increased their stake in tinplate by buying the Eaglesbush. Anyway the whole juggernaught hit the buffers when in 1921; demand vanished. Europe that had stampeded for British products and raw materials had restored their own indigenous industries. Not only did they not want our products but with re-equipped and fully modernised works, the likes of France and Belgium could deliver items such as tinbars into south Wales at below British costs of production. (Affording tinplate works unaffiliated to steel works, which could buy on the open market a fortuitous competitive edge.) Coal suffered a double blow, no longer did the French need our coal and with oil displacing coal, neither did a lot of other people. (Including the Tinplate industry that was converting to gas).

Paradoxically, amongst this gloom, numbers employed now exceeded pre-war levels, mainly due to the introduction of 1st and 2nd helpers. This change to 6-man crews enabled each mill to produce 1000 boxes or more per week, at least equalling the per-mill productivity of almost any foreign tin works. Only Russian works did better, (or claimed to do better!) Unfortunately this increased throughput did not necessarily offset the 50% increase in 'Hot-end' wage bill nor did bumper numbers of employees reflect the level of activity since many were on short-time working.

The formation of Allied Tin Box Makers Limited in 1921 (renamed the following year as the Metal Box Company) presaged a welcome expansion in the domestic canning market, and in 1923 the South Wales Tin Plate Corporation was set up, to represent the industry in the market place and assist with sales. Unfortunately since it was dominated by Richard Thomas it was perceived as representing the interests of Messrs Richard Thomas rather than the industry as a whole thus the other tinplate combines shunned it and the few independent members soon resigned.

Amongst all this Folland of the Grovesend Company boldly bought out the great Dyffryn works at Morriston, the Mardy at Gorseinon and the Dynevor at Ammanford. Curiously within two months he had sold the whole Grovesend group to the Richard Thomas Company converting the latter from a major force in the industry to a dominant one. When in 1924 the industry again became fully employed it seemed that once again the Richard Thomas people had read the omens correctly and that the £1.1 million that they paid for the dozen works of the Grovesend Company was a bargain. In actual fact within a year the slump returned and the Grovesend acquisition took on a millstone-like guise.

Although not perhaps of immediate profit, there was one very positive post-WW1 development, the establishment of the University College of Swansea partly to provide the education and research that the tinplate industry had hitherto lacked. This would eventually feed through giving the tinplate industry a much need professionalism in a time of change and challenge.

Of more immediate benefit were Mr Austin and Mr Morris's motors for the masses, creating a demand for sheet that caused the Llanelli Steel Company to erect a 6-mill sheet works and galvanising plant. Of more import to the actual tinplate side of things was the 1925 joint venture by Baldwins and the Anglo-Persian Oil Company (Later B.P.) to build the magnificent 16-mill Elba tinplate works (Not to be confused with the entirely separate Elba steel works).

The designer/manager of Elba tinplate was S. R. Cound one of the most respected experts in the industry who having learnt the trade at Gorseinon had; a decade earlier designed and commissioned the Moscow Metal Works tinplate works. (This know-how export was repeated half a century later when Trostre men advised on the construction of the Magnitogorsk tinplate works in Siberia. At Elba, Cound put 3 mills in tandem, echoing the work of John Williams of Pontardawe who had experimented with a 4-mill train, thus anticipating the '5-stand' that would become the heart of the Cold Reduction process a quarter of a century later. Elba with the adjacent Baldwins' King's Dock works concentrated on the manufacture of 'Oil plate' – tinplates in sizes and substances to suit the makers of oil and petrol cans. With a works (independently owned) situated in between to make the terne plate boxes for export orders, a virtual 'Industry within an industry' arose.

The 1925 closure by the Richard Thomas Company of their Lydbrook works emphasised the continuing decline of the eastern, off-coalfield works and the concentration that was making Swansea the natural centre of the industry, with most of the works within a 15 miles radius of Swansea docks. Both the Tinplate Association and the Tinplate Conference were Swansea based, with offices in the Swansea Metal Exchange. This building had a Board Room with a remarkable terne plate ceiling, pressed to simulate elaborate plaster moulding, sadly to be lost to enemy action in February 1941.

The Briton Ferry Steel Co further expanded in 1926 by taking over the old Vivian copper works at Port Talbot and installing 3 mills although tinning was never done, only black plate being produced. The motor industry was miniscule by modern standards but its demand for terne plate and black plate was helping to make up for the loss of tinplate business. These products were responsible for the 1927 total tonnage coming within sight of the million, but in a very competitive market the profit potential on both was limited.

In 1928, possibly spurred by signs of an improvement in the tinplate trade, Mrs Leanora Folland the widow of Henry Folland, demonstrated a continuance of her late husband's faith in tinplate by heading a syndicate to open the 3-mill Pencoed works at Bynea. The late 1920s upturn proved regrettably brief and this; the last packmill ever to be built in Britain was sold to Baldwins.

Although the Tregonings at Morfa did invest themselves out of trouble by a major upgrade, Cwmbrwla's closure was more typical of 1929 and was the first of several, as the less economic units succumbed to the chill winds of recession and a blizzard of price cuts. Cilfrew closed the following year, as did the Amman. In

1931 Pentyrch closed, with Dafen giving up tinning to concentrate on their Vitraflex enamelled building products. Remarkably there were something like 75 works still, at least nominally, in business in south Wales only about ten down on the halcyon pre-McKinley days. But certainly by 1931 there was much part-time or intermittent working, with reputedly 7000 tinplate works in south Wales being unemployed.

In 1932 the Tinplate Pooling Scheme was agreed whereby every works other than Elba, (which did not sell on the general market), would limit output to 75% of capacity. Any works fortunate enough to sell more than this quota paid a levy of 2/- (10p) per box into a fund from which works less fortunate in the marketplace could draw the same 2/- per box on their shortfall. There would be a standard price of 15/- (75p) per box, a figure little more than half 1850's prices despite now paying double for tin. There was an inexorable pressure to maximise efficiency to extract any sort of profit at this sort of price level without sacrificing quality. To ensure quality the big users regularly sent inspectors to the works, to take random samples for appraisal at their own laboratories. Relations between the works and these inspectors were invariably cordial and as a matter of courtesy the samples would be taken away to be wrapped whilst the inspectors enjoyed refreshment from the manager's drinks cabinet. Allegedly the wrapped samples returned to the inspectors would be far from random!

In the meantime Sir William Firth now heading the Richard Thomas Company embarked on a buying spree.

In 1933 he bought the Glynbeudy and the Glynrhyd as well as the whole of Gilbertson's Pontardawe interests. The next year he bought Cardonel, Melingriffith and Treforest and in 1935 Bryn and Pencoed, followed in 1936 by Aberdulais, Clayton, Morfa as well as Alyn way out on its own at Mold. This gave the company, besides its steel and coal interests, over 200 tinplate mills.

Metal Box bought Baldwins' temporally idle Eaglesbush not so much as a backward integration of their can-making business, but more to create a centre of excellence to try to improve what they considered to be the variable quality of the tinplate they were buying in. Discomfited by this aspersion on an industry mostly controlled by himself, Firth set up press works at Cwmfelin with some intention of entering the can business. In the event large steel pressings for the motor industry were turned out, enabling the press department to long outlast the rest of the Cwmfelin works. By this time the tinplate quota had been cut to 65% then 55% of capacity. It was not easy to cut down the number of mills, so many such as Ashburnam kept within the quota by working part time or by closing for weeks or months at a time.

The bad state of trade and the virtual disappearance of any profit margin made the 2/- per box payment for effectively not making tinplate, was more attractive than making it. Despite this, in 1933 having been closed for 25 years, Llangennech was reopened, but unsurprisingly it lasted a mere year, and in 1940 the 3 mills, the horizontal compound engine and all the rest of the machinery and tools were sold for scrap.

However even before the first sod had been cut for the Elba works, it and every other tinplate works in the country had been outdated by the Ashland mill in Kentucky. Here, the seemingly immutable two-century old layout of the pack mills had been abandoned. In this new plant steel was cast into ingots, hot-rolled into billets that were then passed through successive stands to be hot-rolled into one long continuous strip that was downloaded as a coil. The strip was cold-rolled through a multi-stand mill to produce material of suitable thickness for tinning. By welding the tail of one coil to the head of the next coil this process could be continuous.

This process increased the per-ton per-man productivity a dozen-fold, the workers never actually handling any material, spending most of the shift sitting at control consoles.

Obviously such a process would never catch on, the product was rubbish, and the trade would never accept it. The position in the market place of the likes of Clayton's 'Best Best Charcoal', and Old Castle's 'Extra Charcoal Killey', was unassailable.

But a chill crept through the boardrooms What if the strip mill product was accepted? What if the trade demanded the larger sheets that the strip process could turn out? The capital cost would be unimaginable. The last big mill to be built the 16-mill Elba had cost £200,000, a plant like the Ashley one would have three times Elba's capacity but would cost thirty times as much (Although this would include steel making). A threefold leap in productivity might make the sums add up, but where would the money come from? The Banks? The Stock

Market? Whilst the returns from working round the clock, might tempt lenders and investors, what if demand fell off? A traditional works could close down mills and lay off the workers, but in such a capital-intensive operation any short-time working would be financially disastrous.

The tinplate industry had lived through an era that had seen the canals come and go, the steam locomotive come and be threatened with extinction. Steamships, motorcars, aeroplanes, electricity, telecommunications and bicycles, had all become commonplace, whilst tinplating was still lodged in the furthest recesses of the eighteenth century when the Mail Coach represented cutting-edge technology. Clearly the industry needed to move forward, but how? As an alternative to the American wide-strip approach, the Germans were developing a much cheaper narrow-strip technique that produced material just wide enough to produce a can but not much good for anything else. Richard Thomas did actually experiment with narrow (8″ wide) strip at the Hendy works, to try out electro-deposition as an alternative to hot dip. It was clearly no more successful than had been an electro-deposition machine dealing in wide (39″) material. That machine worked at Hendy for two years from 1932, then for a further two years at Cwmfelin, but operating at 4″ per minute it would take over 7 hours to coat a box of tinplate!

The 'Tinplate Cartel' of 1934 provided a breathing space. It was agreed a ceiling on exports by Britain, France, Germany and America, a triumph of negotiation particularly by the Welsh delegates, but it was recognised that this could only temporarily stem the advance of the cheaper (and better?) American strip-mill material. Partly as a result of the Cartel it became possible to raise the Pooling prices to 18/9 (94.5p), and for 1936 the quota was increased to 70%, but the industry was still in a 'Damned if they did and damned if they didn't.' situation. Building a strip mill would break any firm that attempted it, not building a strip mill would have much the same result.

Whilst the old 'If it ain't broke (yet!) don't fix it' attitude persisted, John Williams of Pontardawe, W. R. Browne of Old Castle and H. D. Rees of Briton Ferry all pushed for modernisation of the packmill process, possibly taking forward what had been done at Elba. Others such as Sir William Firth of Richard Thomas were adamant that the American pattern had to be followed, and several other steel makers and indeed the Austin motor company had wide-strip proposals of their own.

Richard Thomas now owned more than 45% of the almost 500-mill industry. Baldwins controlled about 7% although its Midlands steel and sheet interests made it a formidable force. The Briton Ferry Company had about 10%, Partridge Jones & John Paton had around 4% with Bynea Group and Upper Forest & Worcester (The latter's 16 mills virtually giving it group status) each having around 3%. The Redbook Tinplate Company operated on 2 sites so they were technically a 'combine' but their 7 mills were small beer. The independent works had around 30%.

The size of a group gave economies in buying, selling, maintenance and administration, but also the size of the works affected efficiency. Supervision and such departments as clerical, maintenance and stores called for almost as many people in a small works as a large one. Also it was claimed that typically 3 boilers could power 12 mills, but it took 2 to power a 6-mill works and that a locomotive would be underemployed in a any works with less than 12 mills. Richard Thomas and Baldwins averaged 7 mills per works, and Briton Ferry just over 5 but although Partridge, Jones & John Paton had the Newport hinterland pretty much sewn up with their more than 20 mills these were dispersed over 6 works so that individual works size was uneconomically small, none having more than 4 mills. As regards the independents half had 4 mills or fewer, thus four fifths of the works (and over 80% of output) was associated with about one fifth of the companies.

Realistically if there was to be a wide-strip mill, since Baldwins only had a minor interest in tinplate, Richard Thomas was the only firm with the expertise and clout to build such a plant. However after Firth's shopping spree Richard Thomas was a huge but cash-strapped monolith and he had to push through a highly controversial scheme of capital reconstruction.

The Government of the day came to the rescue – with strings. They would back Richard Thomas to build a continuous strip mill provided it was not sited in their preferred location, on flat land in north Lincolnshire, close to a port and the Northamptonshire iron mines. It was insisted that any works would have to be erected in an area of high unemployment. Thus this great state-of-the-art project came to be built on the old Ebbw Vale Iron

Works site, which was in a constricted, steep-sided valley remote from any docks; the very sort of location from where the Dowlais Company had fled to Cardiff thirty years before.

Anyway the plant opened in 1938, but the primary reason for siting it in an area of extreme unemployment did not entirely pay off, since most of the unemployed men in Ebbw Vale were colliers and so many of the jobs called for specialist skills that could only be found among steel and tinplate mill men from other places, such as Llanelli and the Swansea Bay area. The sums did not altogether add up either, since the final cost was more than double the original estimate, but the war intervened ditching normal economic criteria and after the war came nationalisation where there were no economic criteria at all. However costs apart, Ebbw Vale was a technical triumph attaining its designed six million box output within 18 months of opening.

Although the standardisation of sizes enforced by strip operation benefited some works able supply customers needing special sizes, Ebbw Vale would soon claim its first packmill victims, Aberdulais and Cambria.

In the meantime things had been moving at Llanelli, Richard Thomas had renovated and reopened the Wellfield works and had increased steel making capacity at the South Wales works, more importantly the Llanelly Steel Company expanded paving the way for the for almost all the tinworks in Llanelli to huddle around it as the Llanelly Amalgamated Tinplate Companies. With only Old Lodge and Pemberton remaining independent, the total of 43 mills of Old Castle, Western, Kidwelly, Teilo and Ashburnham now formed a group on a par with Briton Ferry with an average of over 7 mills per works, with an open-market output greater than Baldwins, capable of absorbing most of Llanelly Steel's tonnage. Everything was within a compact radius close to the docks and to the GWR and LMS main lines, making an enterprise that could be locally described as 'Tidy'. More importantly such a grouping would be strong enough to face up to Ebbw Vale, not perhaps with a full-scale strip mill but able to contemplate improvements on the pack mill process perhaps on the lines of the ideas of W. R. Browne and other influential managers.

Then in 1939 the war came but up to June 1940, the effects were minimal and although the 1937 record output of 20,000,000 boxes, boosted by gasmask canisters, 4-gallon disposable petrol tins and strategic food stockpiling, was a thing of the past it was only after the fall of France, with overseas markets unreachable or taken by the USA under Lease-lend terms, and home demand constrained, most tinplate works went onto short-time or closed. The sheet mills remained busy with orders for heavy-duty sheets for Anderson shelters, Nissan huts and 'Blister' aircraft hangers, the corrugating having been developed at Bryngwyn works; as well as terne plate for millions of 'Jerricans'. This absorbed some tinplate workers but many were directed into munitions factories or to other industries, such as forges in the Midlands.

Of the now idle tinplate works, a number found use as warehouses for food and munitions, providing remote and dispersed locations difficult to bomb at a time when docks and other supply-depots were being singled out for attack. The tinplate owners were praised for their ready co-operation on placing premises at the disposal of the appropriate ministry. Actually of course the opportunity to let and have repaired decrepit premises was a boon. Whilst the rolling departments, designed for heat dispersal rather than security and weatherproofing were usually unsuitable, good use could be made of pickling, cold-rolling, packing and stocking areas. Raven, Amman Dulais, and Glynbeudy, were the first to be used. Morlais at Llangennech was so successful as an Admiralty depot that post-war a permanent complex was built nearby. As dockside warehouses in places such as London and Liverpool were destroyed, surplus areas in active works such as South Wales, Western and Gorseinon were requisitioned. Part of Old Castle became a Bonded Store for tobacco that according to rumour was not a good idea. It is said (untruthfully. I am sure!), that it was possible to access the storage area and that with the vices in the maintenance department serving as presses, quids of tobacco were produced that were eagerly sought-after by the pipe-smokers of Llanelli.

A feature of tinplate working in the 20th century was, by heavy industry standards at least, the high proportion of women. Although far fewer were employed in works in Wales than say America, over 10%of Welsh workers were female. Opening, (the splitting up of packs into individual sheets) was almost exclusively a female job and in the cold rolling department women would predominate with young boy school leavers as 'catchers'. Although no females were employed at the 'Hot End', women might well outnumber the men in the pickling department, which although classed as the part of the 'Cold End' was hot and unpleasant as well as skilled work, so usually older women were employed. Cleaning, assorting and clerical work was also, to use the modern term, 'Unisex'. Since few of the women continued working after marriage almost half were under 20 years of age. Women typically worked from 6 am – 2 pm. Although afternoon overtime might bring extra cash the 11/- (55p) –12/6 (62.5p) that the young girls would take home at the end of the week was not overgenerous even for the times, but these times employers could not afford to be generous.

In all, at the outbreak of WW2 over 4000 women were employed in south Wales tinplate works, with works closed or on short time working, many of these women found themselves out of work.

Thus when the Royal Ordnance Factories of Pembrey, Hirwaun, Bridgend, Cardiff and Glascoed, and the private firms engaged in munitions manufacture commenced recruiting the unemployed tinplate women plus many times that number of retired tinplate women provided a two or even three generation pool of labour used to heavy work in a factory environment. By a marvel of organisation, tens of thousands of women were moved from the valleys to the munitions works. Work was round the clock so that three times per day hundreds of motorbuses travelled in convoys all over south Wales. Scores of special trains to which even expresses had to yield precedence, served Bridgend and Pembrey each having their own stations on the Great Western main line.

Women had worked in various industries in WW1 but this was on a much larger scale. The hours were long, the work arduous and often dangerous, but the pay was liberal. Even where the husbands were not in the forces, wives became the chief breadwinners, indeed teenage daughters might be bringing home more than their coalface worker fathers. All this gave women, particularly young women and independence and a confidence that permanently altered the social fabric of southern Wales.

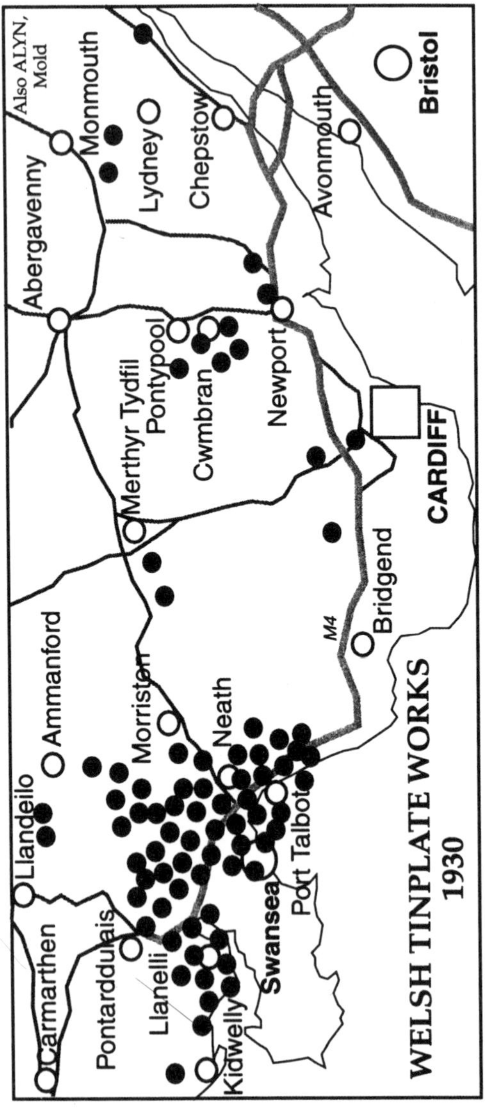

WELSH TINPLATE WORKS
1930

9

Tinplate Post War

World War 2 left Welsh tinplate in a sorry state.

Aber at Llansamlet, Beaufort at Morriston, Bryn at Ynysmedwy, Cardonnel at Skewen, Copper Miners at Cwmafon, Glynbeudy at Brynaman, Raven at Glanaman, Redbrook and Tynewydd in Gwent, Morfa, Old Lodge, South Wales and Western at Llanelli and further west Ashburnham and Kidwelli also Waterloo at Machen and Ynsycedwyn in the Swansea valley, had all closed. Such works as Glanrhyd, Gorseinon and Hendy that had stumbled through the war un-requisitioned, had worn out machinery producing at too high a cost.

Before the war's end the problem of overproduction had been foreseen and it was estimated that little more than two-thirds of the almost 500 mills would ever be used. So it was decided to create the Redundancy Scheme that would permanently scrap 30% of the mills. The amalgamation of Richard Thomas with Baldwins gave them, despite having closed several works, control of over 50% of the pack mill industry. Briton Ferry and Llanelly Associated Tinplate each had just under 10%, Partridge Jones & John Paton had around 5% and Bynea and Upper Forest & Worcester having the same between them. Almost a score of independents, mostly with at best 4 mills, accounted for around 20%. With this imbalance, a 'One size fits all' solution was difficult to come by.

Eventually it was agreed that the groups would reduce their capacity by 25% without compensation, but for each mill scrapped to reduce capacity by up to a further 5% would attract a £5500 payment. The independents would reduce capacity by the full 30% but would get £5500 for each mill scrapped. The idea was good but the practicalities less so. How would a 2-mill works such as Park scrap 30% of its mills? How many would a 4-mill works scrap? It was further agreed that if a small works were withdraw from tinplating altogether by scrapping all its mills it would be paid £7500 for each mill, not bad money for binning an almost non profit-making asset. It was even whispered that some works 'scrapped' mills that were already worn out beyond repair.

RTB closed the 2-mill Ely and all their 3-mill works; Amman, Bryn, Cambria, Cynon, Dynevor, Edlogan, Pencoed and Phoenix as well as all their 4-mill works Alyn (Mold), Cardonnel, Treforest and Wern, the 6-mill Aberdulais as well as the 8-mill Aber. All had been requisitioned for storage other than Wern that had been equipped to make aluminium components for aircraft. RTB later took advantage of the Redundancy Scheme to shut down all 15 tinplate mills at Cwmfelin, and to sterilise 4 of the 15 mills at Dyffryn, 5 of 11 at Lydney and 4 of 12 Melingriffith.

Briton Ferry Steel closed the 4-mill Ferry and Resolven works and the 6-mill Melyn (Transferring the 4 sheet mills to the Neath Steel Sheet & Galvanising Co.) and took out 3 of the 7 mills at Villiers.

Against the trend of closing the smaller works Llanelli Associated Tinplate opted not to re-open the 7-mill Kidwelly and the 6-mill Old Lodge, yet they re-started the 4-mill Ashburnham, one of the few works requisitioned for storage to be re-activated. They also scrapped 7 of the 10 mills at Old Castle.

Partridge, Jones & John Paton, closed the 3-mill Caerleon works and the 4 tinplate mills at Pontymister, the latter one of the few non-requisitioned works to close under the Redundancy Scheme. They also took out 2 of the mills at Pontypool.

Independents such as the (once) 9-mill Beaufort, 8-mill Copper Miners (Cwmafon), 4-mill Dulais, Fairwood, Gyrnos, Morlais, and Ystalyfera, the 3-mill Ynyscedwyn and the 2-mill Park shut up shop altogether, Pemberton ceased tinning but retained the mills to produce black plate. In all less than half the independent works failed to survive the war and its aftermath.

The trade worked out a voluntary levy system for workers that lost their jobs as a result of the closures. This Redundancy Pay Scheme had been worked out well in advance and by a levy of 1d (.4p) per box, a pot of almost a million pounds had been accumulated. A points system was worked out. Service up to the age of 45 earned 1 point per year 46-65 earned 2 points. Rollermen were awarded £2 per point and lesser grades down to £1.10 0 (£1.50) so a top man close to retiring age would get up to about £140. However with the industry regaining some lost overseas markets and the British canned vegetable market explosively expanding, the problem was a shortage rather than a surplus of workers. In fact although the Redundancy programme envisaged an industry of over 300 mills, it was never possible to man even 200, in the less than 40 works that survived. Part of the labour shortage arose from men who had been in the armed forces or had been directed into factory work, having lost the ability to cope with the strains of mill work and part from the reduction of shifts to six hours, but it was in no small measure due to the several schemes for attracting new industry to 'Trading Estates' throughout south Wales, with the intention of providing jobs and hopefully to develop demand for tinplate. This latter goal proved elusive since although the Metal Box Company, the Crown Cork Company and several small canister makers were consumers, the several toy makers' products now tended to be die cast rather than made of the traditional tinplate, but they did provide employment – at pay rates unaffordable and in conditions unattainable, in the tinplate works. Besides this, it took several years to develop the skills needed for the 'Hot end' and with an increased percentage of the workforce now being female, there were fewer vacancies in say the Cold Rolls where a lad would begin to learn the trade. There was no formal training programme, the usual pattern of learning being that school-leaving boys would work in the Cold Roll department, and then hopefully while still under twenty they would move to the mills as Behinders, then work as Second Helpers. Hopefully moving from there to First Helper, then to Furnaceman, then to the exacting and dangerous job of Doubler before reaching the pinnacle of Rollerman.

A nationwide advertising campaign brought in some applicants but most were unsuitable, but for the rest a training scheme was introduced that gave 'In works' training on a wage of £4.00 per week, not exceptional money but enough to be attractive to unskilled men. Unfortunately this wage level proved a little over-generous since having completed a course in one works, trainees tended go to another works and get taken on as a trainee there, thus having a much easier time than actually working! In any case such courses were liable to be treated as a temporary source of income whilst better-paid and lighter work was sought outside the industry. This scheme was extended to attract displaced persons from Eastern Europe, who were brought over and lodged in a hostel at Morriston, but this was often used as an opportunity to get established in Britain, again in order to seek work outside the industry.

More successful was the scheme worked out with the Italian authorities to bring workers over from Italy. The 2000 men that were eventually recruited proved excellent workers, often working back-to-back shifts and even on occasion working three consecutive 6-hour shifts. They were most happily assimilated both into the workplaces and into the communities, in contrast to attempts in Yorkshire to bring them into the coalmines, where they were shunned by the colliers and unions.

Curiously the only antagonism came from their café-owning compatriots. This was due to a tendency to buy a cup of tea and then spend the evening playing cards. Fine in their home villages, but not welcome in a busy, high-rent premises in Morriston or Pontardulais.

When in 1957, the scheme came to an end many of the 1000 Italians then remaining rejected the offer of free passage home, opting to remain in Britain.

In the immediate post-war years, from 1945 onwards, no matter how bravely the tune 'there'll always be a pack mill' was whistled in the dark, the shadow of the continuous strip mill became ever longer. Now, as opposed to the 1930s, there was a joker in the pack, electrolytic tinning a process that did not really lend itself to pack mill working. Developed in the USA to economise on tin, when the Japanese cut off the Malayan supplies, it involved passing the sheet through a stannous electrolyte where clusters of tin anodes passing thousands of amps at perhaps 8 volts deposited a plating of tin – a far cry from the 1930s Hendy and Cwmfelin trials. Tin consumption was reduced from around a pound per basis box of the hot dip process, to a few ounces. Wartime necessity became peacetime economy. Electrolytic tinning could not only apply much tin much more thinly but also the coating thickness could differ on the two sides. This was especially valuable for many canning applications since fruit and fish cans had to be lacquered internally, thus the plating on one side only had to protect the sheet as far as the can factory.

Electrolytic tinplate was dismissed as 'Rustbucket Rubbish', but in fact its inferior corrosion resistance was due to the thinner coating. At equal thickness there was nothing to choose between the two and its adoption by Ebbw Vale in 1947 became the first notable post-war modernisation in the industry.

In 1947 faced with the certainty that very large sums would have to be spent re-equipping the industry a syndicate between Guest Keen & Baldwins, Lysaghts and Llanelli Associated Tinplate was formed, the grandly named Steel Company of Wales.

GKB as well as their Port Talbot and Margam steelworks, tipped in 11 Richard Thomas & Baldwins tinplate works; Burry, Glanrhyd, Gorseinon, Kings Dock, Lydney, Mardy, Melingriffith, and R. T. Mills. Also the tinplate departments of the Dyffryn, Grovesend and Pontardawe works, retaining the steel-making element in each case. They also included the premises of the idle, Hendy, Morfa and South Wales works. Llanelli Associated Tinplate put Ashburnham, Old Castle, Teilo and Western into the pot. Lysaghts having no tinplate works just contributed their Newport electrical steel works.

The first task of this combine was to build a new 'Super works'. Besides supplying tinplate this plant would make the huge tonnages of wide-strip for which the car industry was crying out. Unlike Ebbw Vale this new Abbey works, an add on to the old GKB Port Talbot and Margam works, would have no tinning facilities but would supply steel coil to a separate tinplate works at Velindre that would cold roll the coils from 'Car Body' thickness to 'Can' thickness before electrolytically tinning the coils then chopping them up into sheets.

The cold-reduction strip-mill part of the scheme had stumbled when the siting was switched from Velindre to Trostre, this latter plant starting to come on stream in 1952, giving rise to one pack mill closure, the 11-mill

Morriston & Midland. By 1953 Trostre's output really began to build up causing the closure of 10 works, Aberavon, Ashburnham, Dyffryn, Elba, Ffrwdwyllt, Glanrhyd, Grovesend, Gwalia, Hendy, Villiers and Western, followed the next year by Byass and R. T. Mills, cutting a 90-mill hole in the industry stretching from Burry Port to Port Talbot.

In the meantime in 1951 there had been blanket nationalisation of the whole of the steel industry, followed a bare two years later by de-nationalisation of all of it save RTB. During this brief period the long-discussed matter of pensions was settled by the superannuation scheme set up by the Steel Company of Wales being adopted industry wide. Most of the companies large and small had pension arrangements, but attempts to consolidate these into a blanket plan had always failed. In fact in 1946 when a pension plan was drawn up by the Tinplate Conference it provoked one of the very few strikes to occur in this industry noted for its excellent labour relations.

This partial de-nationalisation meant that the Steel Company of Wales regained its works, as did the Bynea group, with the Albion Steelworks and Llanelly Steelworks being bought by the Midlands-based Duport Company. The independent part of the tinplate industry virtually ceased to exist, leaving almost all the capacity in the hands of two groups S.C.O.W and RTB, with the odd situation of one half of the industry having to make a profit for shareholders whilst the other's losses could be met from the pubic purse!

Despite this handicap, and the threat of renationalisation that affected its capital-raising abilities, the Steel Company of Wales went ahead with the building of Velindre, virtually a 'Carbon copy' of Trostre, thus doubling the firm's tinplate capacity. The closure of Baglan Bay at the end of 1956, almost before Velindre had come fully on stream, presaged the extinction of the traditional tinplate industry.

1957 saw some 100-mills scrapped in a swathe that devastated every tinplate community right from Llanelli to Gloucestershire. The 13-works hit list included the oldest and most famous names in the industry; Abertillery, Clayton, Gorseinon, Kings Dock, Lydney, Mardy, Old Castle, Pemberton, Pontardawe, Pontypool, St David's and Teilo. In addition, Melingriffith (the last tinplate works to use water power) whose remaining 8 mills had been taken on as a stopgap by S.C.O.W. also closed that year.

The next year there was a clean up of some niches the previous year's cull had missed, Avondale, Players and the once mighty Upper Forest and Worcester.

This left just a solitary works at Llanelli, the never-surpassed-in-size Bury, and Glamorgan and Glynhir at Pontardulais. By the end of 1961 these and the 250-year pack mill era were history. The last vestige of the hand-working of sheet came in 1968 with the closure of the Neath Sheet Steel & Galvanising Company, just outlasting the automating of the Neath telephone exchange that ended it's distinctive and memorable telephone number – Neath 1.

Gone was the comradeship that only discomfort and danger can generate, gone were the breakfast bacon and egg fry-ups on a red-hot tinbar and the tea-can stewed on a furnace foreplate. Gone was the pre-dawn ring of boot-nails on the streets of Llanelli, Pontardulais and Morriston; and the salty banter of the girl openers. No longer would gypsies scrounge Wasters to make clothes pegs. Gone too, dare one say, were the surreptitious visits to the works bran-bin, to seek a little treat for one's rabbit.

The Bury and the Elba bereft of their mill-stands and furnaces found brief second careers hot dipping sheet from Trostre while Abertillery and Abercarn fulfilled a similar function for Ebbw Vale. The long closed Cwmbwrla became a central pallet depot for RTB. Other works were retained for packaging or storage. Wern continued in aluminium manufacture for many years, others found re-use. Fairwood became a foundry (Western Light Castings), Caerleon became a shovel works, Dafen became a steel warehouse, Cilfrew an industrial lift factory and Melingriffith housed light industry. Briton Ferry Steel's Baglan Foundry relocated in Melyn when road widening enforced a move and several others housed general engineering workshops. Kidwelly having been a scrap warehouse happily became a notable museum. In the case of other works, the sites have been industrially reused, Aberdulais becoming a bottled gas depot, but most vanished under housing, roads and other radical redevelopments.

In the 1960s, the last hot-dip pots were transferred from Elba to Trostre, to shortly disappear altogether as the mainstream industry went 100% electrolytic. A double-reduction line at Trostre increased both the capacity and the product range. Most coils were being continuously annealed instead of being annealed coil by coil. And after some three centuries of reducing the thickness of tin coating, 'tin free' coating would become a reality. Chromium/Chromic Oxide electrolytically deposited reduced the weight of coat to fractions of grams. Eventually metallic thickness would be reduced to zero with the advent of polymer coating. Increasingly product would be sold in coils, obviating shearing and boxing. New methods would speed up roll servicing; it was 'all systems go'.

Although the use of tinplate for the manufacture of artefacts, and certain containers was being displaced by plastics, consumption of home-canned fruit, vegetables and soups was multiplying. At the same time the real market-driver was pet-food. Only a generation before, anyone enquiring for tinned food to feed a pet would have, at best been advised to seek qualified medical advice. By the 1960s pet food manufacturers were the largest users of tinplate and one of the major markets for steel products as a whole.

Concomitant with this was the growth of canned drinks. Canned beer had been pioneered in the 1935 by Felinfoel Brewery at Llanelli, but the lacquer used was said to affect the taste of the beer and the tapered top can was dearer than its glass equivalent. The cylindrical can was competitive and was made acceptable by the development of the ring-pull in the 1960s and this and the increase in consumption of drinks of every kind should have provided an enormous market for tinplate. Particularly as an increased percentage of drink was not consumed in public houses. In the event plastics took a large proportion of the soft drinks market, and aluminium took much of the rest.

A traditional can is made from three pieces, a rectangle that is rolled around and joined to form a tube and two ends one of which is fitted by the can maker and the other by the filler. The late 1970s invention of the two-piece can revolutionised can making. There are two processes the Drawn and Wall Ironed process used for most cans and the Drawn and Redrawn process used for shallow cans. Both involve deep drawing a flat circle into a cup, to give a product that is cheaper than the body/bottom end combination, particularly as generally thinner material can be used. A further economy is that it is possible to 'neck' beverage cans, reducing the size and hence the cost of the one remaining end.

The bad news is that for the body at least, this process puts aluminium at least head to head with tinplate, and for many purposes offers a cost advantage. Tinplate can still be competitive for the ends but with only one per can required and that possibly reduced in size by necking, little comfort can be derived from this option. Regrettably the indications are that further developments are liable to favour aluminium.

The new Cold Reduction plants were a total change of working environment. Sitting at a console with little noise, no stife, gloom or heat, tinplate work became almost a sedentary occupation. This has brought a possibly unforeseen downside is that there little close contact between men, instead of being jammed together they see little of their colleagues and this coinciding with the car replacing walking or public transport means that many co-workers rarely meet.

Happily, whilst no work can be entirely safe, the accident rate is a fraction of what it once was. Gone is the terrible Doubler's cut where flesh and tendon were sliced and seared to the bone by skidding, blazing-hot sheets, no longer are tinners splashed with molten metal or picklers with acid. No longer do women splitters mar their hands struggling to separate 'stickers'.

Gone too is the dreadful toll of spinning spanners. Despite rules to the contrary, millmen tired of lifting a 20Kg spanner to head height every few minutes to adjust the roll screwdowns, would understandable leave them on the screw's squared end. Usually safe enough, but every now and again vibration or whatever would cause the screwdown to back off whirling the spanner to produce a head-crushing blow, or even throwing it completely off to pole-axe any worker in its path. Gone also are the dreadful crocodile shears, whose relentless jaws could sever fingers or a hand with equal ease.

The aprons and the clogs the doubler's boots, the splitters lead 'palms' and the other self-devised protective items have gone but the modern worker is well garbed. Helmets, high-visibility jackets, ear defenders, goggles, gloves, boots and overalls keep the operators spaceman-secure. Machinery that cannot be adequately fenced has infrared guarding. Sadly also to have gone, are the skills developed and passed down a dozen generations. The craft of the wheelwright, the millwright the mason, the cabinetmaker and a dozen other skills are kept alive by museums and niche markets. Riding, archery, boating and other sports maintain further skills, but now virtually every skill, art and artifice used in traditional tinplate making has been lost forever.

During much of the 20th century the percentage of artefacts being made from tinplate decreased, but the sheer numbers of artefacts ensured a rising demand for tinplate. Such conditions no longer apply.

In addition the manufacture of tinplate at one time needed a heavy engineering ambiance, hence its production was confined to developed nations. Not only are there more such nations, but also paradoxically as tinplate manufacture has become technically more sophisticated, it has become simpler to set up. With standardised equipment and turnkey technology, the likes of Messrs Wean or Head Wrightson can set up a works in a jungle or a desert.

When the pack mills succumbed to the strip mills, there was a domino effect across South Wales starting with the swathe of Siemens Open-hearth steel works finding themselves without customers. Briton Ferry closed in 1950, steel making at Upper Forest & Worcester outlasted the 'Ferry' by just one year. Steel making ended at Bryngwyn in 1951 although it enjoyed a 'Second career' as a coatings plant. Grovesend and South Wales ceased in 1958, and Dyffryn in 1961 closely followed by Bynea and Elba, but automobile steels kept Pontardawe going until

1968 and Albion's diversification kept it in the steel business until 1978. Llanelli made an extensive and expensive conversion to the then fashionable electric arc mini steelworks, only to find the whole of its plant exported a few years later.

The servicing industries such as steel founders Millbrook and Glanmorfa lost their market for rolls and stands, the modern multi-million pound lines are standard, off-the-shelf items, factory built for a world market. Specialist repair works such as Taylor & Sons at Briton Ferry, Thomas & Clement at Llanelli or Warwill's at Abertillery have suffered a triple whammy of the loss of steelworks and collieries, as well as their tinplate works customers. The box makers had to shut up shop, docks closed and clog makers vanished along with all the little stockists and works furnishers. The tin-brokers frenetic Friday lunchtimes, when the Spot Prices having been declared, orders for the coming week were placed; became history.

It was not all bad, with the 'strip mills' seeking to sell in larger and larger quantities, small orders and special sizes would increasingly be dealt with by independent merchants. With homemade protective clothing giving way to factory-made safety-wear, making and distributing these would give business and employment opportunities.

The late 20th century has seen the razing of Velindre in 1981 followed by the total closure of the whole of the integrated Ebbw Vale works, leaving the sheep that once subsisted on discarded sandwiches and welsh cakes in the warmth of the void beneath the great open-heart furnaces, to fend for themselves.

Trostre (and the rump of British Steel) still continues, to first amalgamate with Koninklijke Hoogovens to form Corus, then, just into the 21st century become part of the Indian Tata group.

Tinplate & Sheet Works

Siemens Steel Works supplying Tinbars

(Including steel departments of tinplate works)

(Did not all operate at the same time)